I SEE DEAD PEOPLE

THE MAKING OF
THE SIXTH SENSE

MACKENZIE NICHOLS

APPLAUSE
THEATRE & CINEMA BOOKS

Essex, Connecticut

APPLAUSE
THEATRE & CINEMA BOOKS

An imprint of Globe Pequot, the trade division of
The Rowman & Littlefield Publishing Group, Inc.
4501 Forbes Blvd., Ste. 200
Lanham, MD 20706
www.rowman.com

Distributed by NATIONAL BOOK NETWORK

Library of Congress Cataloging-in-Publication Data

Names: Nichols, Mackenzie, author.
Title: I see dead people : the making of 'The sixth sense' / Mackenzie
    Nichols.
Description: Essex, Connecticut : Applause, [2023]
Identifiers: LCCN 2023008927 (print) | LCCN 2023008928 (ebook) |
    ISBN 9781493072286 (paperback) | ISBN 9781493072293 (epub)
Subjects: LCSH: Sixth sense (Motion picture) | Shyamalan, M. Night |
    Fantasy films—United States—History and criticism.
Classification: LCC PN1997.S5155 N53 2023 (print) | LCC PN1997.
    S5155 (ebook) | DDC 791.43/72—dc23/eng/20230424
LC record available at https://lccn.loc.gov/2023008927
LC ebook record available at https://lccn.loc.gov/2023008928

Printed in India

For my Grandfather, H. Brian Thompson.
Everything I do is to make you proud.

Contents

Introduction

Every once in a while, a film is meant to become a cultural phenomenon. It's meant to shake up Hollywood. It's meant to stand the test of time. From *Forrest Gump*'s "Run, Forrest, Run," to *Star Wars: The Empire Strikes Back*'s "I am your father," some cinematic lines are just meant to become part of our daily vernacular, so recognizable that it's impossible for someone to not understand the references. *The Sixth Sense* was one of those movies. M. Night Shyamalan, legendary filmmaker and philanthropist, started writing the screenplay in his mid-twenties and was so confident in it that he dropped everything and went out to Los Angeles to give the script to all of the studios in Tinseltown. He bought an expensive hotel room and traveled to Hollywood Pictures, New Line Cinema, Columbia Pictures, and Dream-Works, dropping off his screenplay and demanding $1 million for the picture, with him attached as director.

To his surprise, all of the studios were interested, starting a bidding war that would end with Disney's Hollywood Pictures signing off on a $2.5 million bid, a massive bid that would shock Hollywood and change the game for the industry. Shyamalan got what he wanted and more, the universe's way of solidifying the young filmmaker as a force to be reckoned with. Joe Roth, who was chairman of Disney at the time, told me that the undertaking was smooth and successful all the way through. He knew when he read the script that the story was something special. For a man who reads 300 screenplays a year, this means something.

"Everything just lined up and turned out to do great," Roth said. "Most scripts you read aren't good. Even some of the good ones aren't even good. And then every once in a while, you read a great script. And this was a great script."

The pieces that needed to be put into place in order for *The Sixth Sense* to be truly successful started fitting together soon after Shyamalan signed on with Hollywood Pictures. Bruce Willis, a legend in his own right, wanted the part of Dr. Malcolm Crowe even though it was a departure from his usual action roles such as in *Pulp Fiction* and the *Die Hard* franchise. Having this star attached would surely bring in more viewers. The casting process went smoothly, too, with Haley Joel Osment coming in for an audition and knocking it out of the park. (Speaking of *Forrest Gump*, the young actor was actually in that movie for a short amount of time, playing Forrest's son.) Toni Collette, fresh off of *Muriel's Wedding*, appealed to Roth, Shyamalan, and Willis for the part of Lynn Sear. Donnie Wahlberg was so dedicated to his role that he showed up to auditions practically emaciated as Dr. Crowe's estranged patient. Olivia Williams and Mischa Barton then signed on for the smaller roles. Shyamalan had his cast of characters with Willis and Osment leading the way. The young filmmaker was confident that the movie would make waves.

The shooting process went without a hitch with the cast claiming that Shyamalan is a director who knows what he wants out of each shot. Even though he may seem lackadaisical, bouncing a basketball as he sits in the director's seat, he goes into each scene with a clear picture of what he wants out of each actor. He worked one-on-one with every actor, telling Osment to access emotions of fear rather than sadness and urging Collette to treat her relationship with Osment as a kind of partnership, a friendship, almost, rather than a typical mother-son connection.

"Even during scenes I wasn't in, I'd be on set watching him work. I observed as the meticulous storyboards that wrapped around the production office turned into beautifully crafted shots. I was so impressed by the choreographed camera moves and the long takes that Night is renowned for," said Spencer Treat Clark, who played Joseph Dunn in *Unbreakable* and again in *Glass*, both created by Shyamalan.

The reception of *The Sixth Sense* was shocking to the cast and crew even though they were sure it would succeed. Nothing prepared them for how successful the film would be. It rivals the older Hitchcock and Kubrick films, with the young director wanting to tell a simple story without the use of CGI or complicated storylines. It's like a longer *Twilight Zone* episode, a simple premise played by a small group of actors. A young boy goes about his life with a special power: he can see the dead. Shyamalan, who was twenty-nine when the film was released, became a household name by the time he was thirty. Directors like Steven Spielberg took notice of the filmmaker's talent, and soon, Shyamalan would be making more movies with twist endings to try to catch the success again. He would only find this one more time with *Signs* featuring Mel Gibson and Joaquin Phoenix, but throughout his career since, he has not put out something of *The Sixth Sense*'s caliber.

"It's fascinating to think that [the cast and crew] were completely unaware of just how creepy their performances and the movie were for anyone sitting down to watch it. In many ways, that is part of why the film is effective. It takes heavy subjects like grief and death and filters them through the lens of horror in order to make a movie that scares just as much as it packs an emotional punch," wrote film critic Roger Ebert in 1999.

In this book, I dive into the making of *The Sixth Sense*, using exclusive interviews from Shyamalan, Osment, Barton, Roth, Michal Bigger, and more. The book looks at twist endings as a phenomenon in Hollywood, with *The Sixth Sense* as a major tentpole for this kind of filmmaking. I discuss paranormal experiences as a whole and how the craze amplified after *The Sixth Sense* was released in 1999. The picture, at the end of the day, is a classic film, one that changed the industry and made Shyamalan a household name.

"*The Sixth Sense* was the movie that didn't have the legacy to deal with. It didn't have my name to deal with. So, it would be interesting if *The Sixth Sense* was the third movie or the fourth movie and how that would've changed the audience's relationship to the film. Could you even watch the movie? Or would you from the first moment in the movie go, 'Oh, I know what's happening,'" Shyamalan told me. "It's a really interesting thing. That movie created a relationship with my name and then the name itself now has a framing for all the rest of its cousins. It's the one movie that got to live without my name."

1

A Script with Shock Value

M. Night Shyalaman, a horror ingenue with a knack for plot twists, started writing *The Sixth Sense* when he was twenty-five years old, in the mid 1990s. Still a young gun in the industry with a few titles under his belt, he was known for his 1998 comedy *Wide Awake* and an adaptation of *Stuart Little*. Both films struggled to make waves when they first came out, causing the filmmaker to be wary of his writing. "Oh God, it was a long process of writing it," Shyamalan told me. What started as a career in comedy/children's flicks turned into a much different repertoire, and when Shyamalan started working on *The Sixth Sense*, he found that low-budget supernatural mysteries and dramas were more in his wheelhouse. *The Sixth Sense* was surely much different than what he had been working on, delving into the horror genre which he would later be known for.

A young Shyamalan, who at the time was living with his wife and young daughter in Philadelphia, sat clacking away at the script in the nineties and at first, it was meant to be a drama similar to *The Silence of the Lambs* with Jodie Foster and Anthony Hopkins. The terrifying flick, released in 1991, follows FBI agent Clarice Starling as she interacts with and interrogates cannibal killer Dr. Hannibal Lecter in order to find a serial killer named Buffalo Bill, who holds women captive in a hole found in his basement. In comparison to other horror films of the time, *The Silence of the Lambs* was more of a slow drama rather than a fast-paced slasher film like *Halloween* and *Texas Chainsaw Massacre*, focusing on the relationship between Starling and Dr. Hannibal Lecter instead of, say, Freddie Krueger running around slashing up the main characters in the eighties movie *A Nightmare on Elm Street*. The script for *The Silence of the Lambs* is a slow burn, haunting and downright creepy, with memorable lines: "Hello, Clarice" spoken by Hopkins and, "It puts the lotion in the basket" said by Ted Levine (who played serial killer Buffalo Bill) holding just as much power as the line, "I see dead people" spoken by Haley Joel Osment in the final version of Shyamalan's script for *The Sixth Sense*.

In the first draft of the script for *The Sixth Sense*, Shyamalan wrote Bruce Willis's character Dr. Malcolm Crowe as a crime photographer rather than a child psychologist. In this version, Crowe's son has visions of the victims which would presumably help the photographer crack cases. Ten drafts later, Dr. Crowe morphed into a child psychologist who treats Cole Sear, played by Haley Joel Osment, a young boy who has close encounters of the fifth kind as he communicates with and sees the dead.

At the start of the film we see Crowe and his wife, Anna Crowe, played by Olivia Williams, at home in Philadelphia, Shyamalan's hometown, as they are reminiscing and celebrating Crowe's latest award for working closely with mentally ill children. The couple is very much in love, sharing affection and mutual respect. Crowe and his wife sit on the couch in their living room canoodling as Crowe holds his award, proud of his accomplishments and in awe of his supportive spouse, who loves him even if she thinks that she is second in priority compared to his work. As they retire to bed, the two notice that the window in their bedroom is shattered with sharp shards of glass covering the floor. They look at each other in disbelief and Crowe suddenly hears commotion in the bathroom.

That's when Vincent Gray, an estranged patient, appears dressed in just his tighty whities in the restroom, sobbing and grasping a gun in one hand. In the final draft of the script, Shyamalan adds a description of the man, a nineteen-year-old, drugged out, scarred up ex-patient, with a "white patch in his hair," a distinct feature which we'll see later on in Cole Sear's physical description.

Dr. Crowe, an expert in his field, tries to diffuse the situation by telling the young man that there are no needles or prescription drugs in the house, thinking that robbery must be the reason why this disgruntled man has broken into his home. Gray is not there for that. He's there for revenge, he's there for blood, he's there because, as Shyamalan says in the script, Crowe did not "cure" him as a patient, and here Gray is, pointing a gun to the doctor's face.

At this point in the script, Dr. Crowe suddenly remembers Gray from nearly a decade ago, although it takes a few tries to pin down the name.

"I do remember you, Vincent. You were a good kid. Very smart, quiet, compassionate, unusually compassionate," Crowe tells Gray.

This does not help, and Gray responds: "You forgot cursed. You failed me."

Gray, played by Donnie Wahlberg, is emaciated and sobbing, totally out of control. Wahlberg plays the character as completely unhinged. He is spitting at the mouth. He is shaking. He is crying. He's nearly naked. He looks like a malnourished homeless man.

No matter what Dr. Crowe says, it seems that Gray has made up his mind and he shoots the doctor, who falls on the bed, hit by a bullet and bleeding profusely from his abdomen. Anna rushes to his side to try to apply pressure to the wound. Shyamalan uses a bird's eye shot to show Malcolm sputtering and coughing. The scene ends with Anna frantically trying to stop the bleeding. We then see Gray again, briefly, as he puts the gun to his own head and pulls the trigger, ending his own life in Crowe's bathroom.

In these first couple of scenes, we are hit with a massive blow to the main character, and as the story progresses, we are convinced that our protagonist survived the shot. He appears in the next scene and throughout the rest of the movie without bloody clothes and without a bullet wound. We are sure that Willis's Malcolm Crowe is a real, living, breathing person for the remainder of the movie.

"Two years later," the script says, and Shyamalan brings us to a new chapter in Crowe's life, where the doctor sits on a bench in the middle of fall Philadelphia, analyzing his notes about young, eight-year-old Cole Sear, who, according to the notes, was referred to him in September 1998.

"Acute anxiety, socially isolated, possible mood disorder, parent status—divorced, communication difficulty between mother-child," Crowe reads in his notes.

Sear is similar to Vincent Gray, it seems, especially given the child's "possible mood disorder." Shyamalan even goes so far as to describe Cole Sear with a white patch of hair, just like Gray. Crowe follows Sear and studies him from afar until he approaches the young boy who is playing with toy soldiers in one of the pews at a local church.

Approaching the child, he sits next to him and points out Cole's "comically large" glasses, which Sear says belonged to his father. Crowe gathers that Cole must be wearing these glasses because he misses his father, who left him and his mother after their divorce. Although this may be unspoken in the script, the soft, gentle way Willis speaks to the boy shows that the doctor is compassionate, trying to understand the boy in order to help him through his trauma and anxiety. This is a huge departure from Willis's other roles, usually playing a tough guy in action films like *Die Hard* and *12 Monkeys*. Shyamalan continues to characterize Sear, writing that the doctor sees visible cuts and bruises on the boy's arm, indicating that he is dealing with his trauma by harming himself.

"Cole's arms are covered in tiny cuts and bruises. Some almost healed. Some fresh," Shyamalan writes.

The two start to develop a relationship which Sear is curious about, asking Crowe, "Are you a good doctor?" to which Dr. Crowe responds, "I got an award once. From the mayor." This makes Sear more comfortable with him, and the two decide to meet again.

In the next few scenes, we see Crowe's home life with his wife, Anna, played by Olivia Williams. We are given a taste of his failing marriage as Crowe is always working and never home to spend time with his spouse. At this point in the script, we see Anna sleeping on the couch, watching their old wedding tape. The two do not have face-to-face dialogue, with Crowe coming home and venturing into the basement where he has an office, case files, and a tape recorder where he can listen to past sessions with his patients.

Shyamalan then moves to Cole Sear's home life, the two main characters mirroring each other as both deal with communication issues with the ones they love. We meet Lynn Sear, Cole's mother, played by Toni Collette. She is fishing through her laundry and getting Cole ready for school with a bowl of Cocoa Puffs. At this point, Cole is keeping a big secret from his mother. He does not know how to tell Lynn that he can see and speak with the dead and that ghosts are around him at all times. His mother has no idea that her son is dealing with this. We assume that Lynn wants Cole to work with a child therapist to understand why he is so shy and friendless at his elementary school. In reality, the kid is dealing with a unique situation, a paranormal affliction that normal kids don't have to endure.

After Lynn gets done with the laundry, she enters the kitchen. When she walks in, she sees her son sitting flabbergasted and visibly shaken in front of his bowl of cereal. Lynn gasps and is in shock when she realizes that all of the kitchen drawers and cabinets are open. She looks at Cole and then at the cabinets and is terrified, not sure how to explain what she sees. Cole, though, knows exactly what did it: poltergeists and ghosts. He does not share this knowledge with his mother, though. Instead, he says he was looking for

Pop Tarts and that's why the cabinets were all open. But how can an eight-year-old boy open all the cabinets, some not easy to reach, in the span of seconds? The two are stunned and the poor boy is "shaken," as Shyamalan writes. Suddenly, the doorbell rings. Cole's school bully, played by Trevor Morgan, is ready to walk with him to school. Shyamalan adds in his notes that as the boy leaves, his mother notices "two tiny hand prints of sweat" which had formed where Cole had placed his hands on the table, showing his anxiety and discontent. This poltergeist sequence is our first indication that *The Sixth Sense* is a supernatural film, and is the first sign that Cole is troubled by his gift.

Back home after a day of bullying and boredom at his elementary school, Cole finds his mother and Dr. Crowe sitting in the living room. Cole looks at both of them, and Lynn Sear asks if he had a good day at school. The boy shrugs. She then leaves to make the boy pancakes, an after-school treat. Cole and Dr. Crowe are then left in the living room, and Crowe decides to play a game with Cole to break the ice and get the session going.

"How about we play a game first?" Crowe says. "It's a mind-reading game. . . . Did I mention I can read minds? Here's the game. I'll read your mind. If what I say is right, you take a step towards the chair. If I'm wrong, you take a step back towards the doorway. If you reach the chair, you sit. If you reach the door, you can go. Deal?"

Cole obliges and the game begins, Cole standing timidly close to the front door. Crowe guesses first that Cole's mother went to see a psychologist after her divorce, but the doctor didn't help her. Because of this, Crowe guesses that Cole now believes that Dr. Crowe won't be able to help the Sear family either. Crowe is right, and Cole steps forward to the chair. In this sequence, the viewer starts to learn about the boy's past traumas, building a strong relationship between Cole and Dr. Crowe.

Crowe then guesses correctly that Cole has a deep secret that even his mother doesn't know and Cole takes a step forward. They do not delve into the secret at this point, but keep continuing the game. Crowe guesses that Cole has never gotten into serious trouble, but Cole then takes a step backward and explains why.

"We were supposed to draw a picture. Anything we wanted," Cole says. "I drew a man. He got hurt in the neck by another man with a screwdriver."

Crowe asks Cole if he saw that on television, and the boy takes a step backwards to the door, indicating that the doctor guessed wrong. The child must have seen the gruesome image from somewhere else. At this point, Shyamalan is breadcrumbing the viewer, slowly but surely hinting that Cole can see the dead. Crowe hasn't caught on yet. The doctor loses the game. Crowe failed this time, but he does not give up on Cole like he did to Vincent Gray. He wants to help the child. He wants to uncover the child's well-kept secret. He will, in time, and until then, trust has to be built between the two protagonists.

As the movie progresses, we learn more about Cole's gift. In one scene, the boy's teacher, Mr. Cunningham, is teaching the children about the history of Philadelphia, specifically delving into the school's history.

"Can anyone guess what this building was used for a hundred years ago, before you went here, before I went to this school even?"

Cole raises his hand.

"They used to hang people here," the eight-year-old says. Mr. Cunningham is shocked at the child's response. He says that this is incorrect, but Cole persists. He is sure that he is right.

"They'd pull the people in crying and kissing their families bye. . . . People watching would spit at them."

"Cole, this was a legal courthouse. Laws were passed here. Some of the first laws of this country. This building was full of lawyers," Mr. Cunningham argues back.

"They were the ones who hanged everybody," Cole says.

At this point, the rest of the class is stunned, including the teacher. They all give Cole confused and concerned looks, and the distressed young boy says, "I don't like people looking at me like that."

Then, he decides to single the teacher out, calling him a "stuttering Stanley," a name that Cunningham received from peers when he was in school. How would this boy know that about him? The teacher is dismayed. He starts to stutter, becoming ashamed, angry, and confused all at once. The energy of the room is palpable and Cole starts screaming, "Stuttering Stanley! Stuttering Stanley!"

The energy of the room becomes frantic. The camera pans upward to the teacher who is shocked that Cole knew about his speech impediment from childhood, and as Cole yells, the teacher does, in fact, start stuttering. In Shyamalan's notes, he writes, "Mr. Cunningham's expression drains of anger as Cole Sear begins to cry."

Shyamalan, through his script, shows the viewer just how much Cole's gifts affect him.

In a later scene, Cole is invited to a birthday party, where bullies lock him in a crawl space and Cole bangs against the door, screaming at the top of his lungs. Lynn, who is downstairs, starts asking where Cole is and then hears the screaming, running upstairs to save the boy. She is so worried about him as she sees the boy shaking that she decides to take him to a doctor for fear that Cole had a seizure while in the crawl space. The two then leave for the hospital and Cole is taken to a pediatrician, who says, "The tests indicate he did not have a seizure. In fact he's doing fine. After some rest, he could go home tonight."

Crowe and Lynn Sear are both sitting, listening to the doctor, played by Shyamalan himself. He expresses concern about the cuts and bruises on Cole's arms, insinuating that Lynn may have hurt her son. At this point, she still does not realize that Cole may be engaging in self-harm.

Cole stays the night in the hospital with Crowe at his bedside. The doctor tells the boy a bedtime story and suddenly, Cole stops him. His blankets are up to his neck. He is distraught and now, he feels ready to open up to Crowe about his deepest, darkest secret. Crowe feels the same. The doctor tells Cole that he is having troubles with his wife and also discusses his ex-patient Vincent Gray, who reminds Crowe of Cole.

"I want to tell you my secret now," Cole says. This is the moment that changes the rest of the movie and turns it from just a drama into a full blown paranormal horror flick. Shyamalan writes, "Cole takes an eternal pause. A silent tension engulfs them both."

"I see dead people . . . some of them scare me," Cole finally says.

"In your dreams?" Crowe responds.

Cole shakes his head.

"When you're awake?"

Cole nods. "Walking around, like regular people, . . . They can't see each other. Some of them don't know they're dead. They tell me stories . . . things that happened to them. . . . Things that happened to people they know."

"How often do you see them?" Crowe asks.

"All the time. They're everywhere," Cole responds.

At this point, Crowe believes that Cole is suffering from hallucinations, paranoia, and schizophrenia, but as the movie continues, the doctor is convinced that his mediumship is legit.

Cole's return from the hospital is a turning point in the film, where it shifts from an emotional drama into a more gruesome thriller. Although it doesn't get as gory or bloody as other eighties and nineties horror movies such as *Halloween*, *Seven*, and *Friday the 13th*, the few violent scenes that Shyamalan does write and direct are still effective in scaring the audience.

When Cole has to use the bathroom in the middle of the night, he runs down the hallway to get to his destination as soon as possible. He makes it to the bathroom and turns on the light, giving him some peace of mind. Shyamalan writes, in all capital letters, "A LARGE FIGURE MOVES PAST THE DOORWAY." Here we go, into the thick of Cole's "hallucinations." The thermostat shows that it's 52 degrees. Ghosts, according to many mediums and paranormal investigators, have the power to manipulate temperature, leaving rooms freezing. This is an indication that Cole is, in fact, not alone in the hallway.

Cole decides to investigate the house to see if there is anyone there besides him and his mother. He makes it to the kitchen and sees a woman standing above a pot on the stove. He thinks it is his mother and says, "Momma, dream about Daddy again?"

In this scene, Shyamalan brings us into Cole's world, revealing the first full-bodied apparition covered in blood.

"The person turns. It's not Lynn," Shyamalan writes. "It's a strange woman. The woman's face is demented. A purple gash cuts across her forehead. All the cabinets and drawers are open behind her."

The woman rushes toward Cole, exposing her wrists, which have been badly cut. Shyamalan fixes the camera panned upward at the woman from Cole's perspective, showing that this ghost is towering over the boy. It's the same kind of shot that Shyalaman uses with Cole's teacher Mr. Cunningham, shot as if Cole is holding the camera himself. These shots are effective because we can really see what Cole's eight-year-old eyes see, physically putting us in Cole's shoes. Cole retreats, running toward his makeshift tent which has the words "Do not touch" on it. He has religious images and figurines inside the tent to bring him protection and peace.

In a next scene, after Cole participates in a school play, Crowe is there in the back of the auditorium and follows the boy outside into a corridor of the school after the play is finished. Cole sees something that Crowe doesn't see, three bodies hanging by ropes at the end of the corridor.

"The ropes and school banners dangling at the top of the stairs sway a little. . . . But so do the three bodies hanging by their necks from a wooden beam," Shyamalan writes. "It's truly a horrific sight. A black man in britches and no shirt, face beaten to a pulp, hangs in the center. A white woman in a torn white frilly dress—tears soaking her face, hangs to the right. A small mixed race child in half pants, hangs to the left. The family stares at Cole. They follow Cole with their tortured eyes as he exits the stairwell."

We are now undoubtedly shocked and sympathetic to the boy's plight that he has to see these cadavers all the time, without being able to share his experiences with friends and family, just Crowe. One of the most disturbing elements of horror films is seeing actors hanging from ropes in apparent suicide. It is rare in film to see such atrocity. When we see actors hanging like this in *The Sixth Sense*, it harkens back to films such as *Suspiria*, *The Omen*, *Scream*, and *House*, each time totally disturbing us perhaps even more so than stabbings, shootings, and suffocations. In *House*, we see an elderly woman hanging by suicide at the start of the film, setting off the horror with a bang. In *The Omen*, a woman hangs herself in an early scene, jumping off the balcony after praising Damien, a young boy who we later find out is the spawn of Satan. In *Suspiria*, a woman hangs by a rope while also covered in blood. Shyamalan uses suicide by hanging in *The Sixth Sense* as an easy way to disturb and freak us out, and he succeeds.

In a later paranormal scene at the Sear house, Lynn accuses Cole of stealing his late grandmother's bumblebee pendant and putting it in Cole's bedside drawer. At this point, Cole is sure that his dead grandmother put it there, not him. He tells his mother that it was not him who moved the broach. Lynn doesn't believe him. This would have been another opportunity for the boy to tell his mother about his secret, but he holds back and still keeps it to himself.

Shyamalan hits us with more gore in the next scene. Cole sees a boy, a few years older than him, in his doorway. The boy says, "Come on . . . I'll show you where my dad keeps his gun."

As the boy turns, Cole sees that he has a hole in his head where a bullet wound has left a pool of blood on the ghost boy's matted hair.

"Cole is too terrified to move," Shyamalan writes.

After his initial shock, he then runs to his mother, asking to sleep in her bed. She agrees and asks her son, "What's wrong?"

This is another moment that could have been an opportunity for Cole to tell his mother what he is seeing. He, again, stays silent.

Meanwhile, Crowe's wife, who works at an antiques and jewelry shop, interacts with a man who Crowe sees from the window. He suspects that his wife is having an affair. He tells Cole in a later scene, "My goal is to speak to my wife. The way she and I used to speak. Like there was no one else in the world but us." The passion he feels for his wife is notable and relatable and almost keeps Crowe from working with Cole moving forward.

"I haven't given my family enough attention. Bad things happen when you do that. Do you understand?"

"Don't fail me," Cole says in response to Crowe telling him that he would be transferred to another doctor.

Crowe, shocked, is undoubtedly brought back to what Vincent Gray told him before he shot the doctor in the abdomen, when the man told Crowe that he had failed him. The parallels of Gray and Cole are apparent in Shyamalan's screenplay. Crowe is determined to not fail the child like he failed Gray previously.

Later, Crowe and Cole are in the church again, and Crowe asks Cole what he thinks the ghosts want from him.

"Just help," Cole says.

Crowe agrees, "Even the scary ones."

Cole is thrilled that Crowe believes him.

"I think they know you're one of those rare people who can see them. You need to help them. Each one of them. Everyone wants to be heard. Everyone," Crowe says.

Cole asks Crowe if he's sure that they want help. He is insecure in this belief. He feels that some are just out there to hurt other people.

"I don't think that's the way it works, Cole," Dr. Crowe says.

This scene is a set up for a young Mischa Barton to appear in ghost form as deceased girl Kyra Collins in Cole's tent late one night. She appears to Cole because she needs his help, just as Dr. Crowe predicted.

Barton enters the scene, sitting before him spewing vomit from her mouth, terrifying the young boy and the viewer, too. She is one of the ghosts who needs help. She is emaciated, "withered," as Shyamalan writes in his notes.

Cole quickly darts away from the tent to meet his dog, Sebastian, down the hall in the living room. After a beat, Cole gathers the courage to venture back into his tent, where Kyra is still sitting, vomiting.

"Do you want to tell me something?" Cole asks. Now, he is ready to face the ghosts and use his gift to help them find peace in their afterlife. He wants to help Kyra instead of running away from her like he does with other apparitions.

The next day, we follow Crowe and Cole to Kyra's funeral. The bus ride is long, but Crowe and Cole are determined to help the dead girl at all costs. When they arrive, they see Kyra's family members and friends dressed in black, mourning the loss of the eight-year-old girl. Crowe and Cole see a four-year-old girl on a swing and presume that she is Kyra's little sister. She looks just as frail as her older sibling.

Visitors' conversations are overheard, and we learn that Kyra had been sick in bed for six years and her younger sister is also ill.

Cole and Crowe decide to sneak upstairs to investigate Kyra's room for any clues as to how they can help Kyra move into the afterlife. Suddenly, "an emaciated hand," presumably Kyra's, emerges from beneath the bed, grabbing Cole's ankle.

In Shyamalan's screenplay, he writes in his notes that Kyra "thrusts a jewelry box forward" for Cole and Crowe to find. This is how Cole can help her find peace, by investigating the contents of the jewelry box. In it, Cole and Crowe find a videotape.

The duo ventures back downstairs to find Kyra's father, Mr. Collins, and Cole hands him the jewelry box.

"It's for you. . . . She wanted to tell you something."

In Shyamalan's notes, he writes, "The father becomes very still. His eyes fill with a storm of confusion and pain."

In the box rests a videotape, unlabeled.

Mr. Collins takes the tape out of the box and puts it into the television and soon all of the attendees are viewing what seems to be a play put on by Kyra with her puppets before she dies. She is happily playing with the dolls in her room. Kyra's dad smiles as he watches. Then, her mother appears in the frame, bringing the girl her lunch, a bowl of soup and sandwich. Mr. Collins, confused, watches his wife pour a bottle of floor cleaner into the soup.

Kyra asks, "Can I go outside, if I eat this?"

Her mother replies, "We'll see. You know how you get sick in the afternoon."

The viewer, upon watching what just took place, realizes that the mother had been poisoning Kyra and keeping her sick. This moment of Munchausen by proxy is stark and heartbreaking. By this point, we have not really seen many storylines about the disease which causes mothers or caretakers to poison loved ones in order to keep them controlled and sick. *The Act*, a Hulu show released in 2019 featuring Patricia Arquette and Joey King, tells the true story of Dee Dee Blanchard poisoning her daughter Gypsy, keeping her sick until Gypsy and her boyfriend killed her in 2015. Other films with storylines about the illness include *Phantom Thread*, *Ma*, and

Everything, Everything, in the 2010s. *The Sixth Sense* was one of the first films to depict the illness, with its popularity in storylines only hitting the mainstream in recent years.

After Mr. Collins realizes that his wife was keeping his daughter sick, Shyamalan writes, "Soon, tears begin flooding Mr. Collins' eyes."

"Don't say [the food] tastes funny. You know I don't like to hear that," Mrs. Collins says in the video.

Mr. Collins approaches his wife. "You were keeping her sick," he says.

"The whole world stops," Shyamalan writes. "Rage is filling every cell of his body. Tears falling faster down his cheeks."

At this point, we are convinced that the mother has been poisoning Kyra's little sister, too. The whole room is stunned as the camera pans around the living room, stopping to catch a glimpse of Kyra's mother, who is looking around at the guests' faces, all in complete dismay and hatred for what Mrs. Collins had done to her daughters.

On the way out of the funeral, Cole approaches Kyra's little sister and hands her a finger puppet, a sort of token of consolation. Crowe and Cole leave the funeral without a doubt that they helped Kyra move on and find peace.

In a more wholesome scene, Shyamalan writes Cole playing a major part in his school play. He sits in the makeup room, talking to a ghost who is "grotesquely disfigured." She recognizes Mr. Cunningham, who appears in the room, saying, "Poor Stanley. My favorite student," before retreating into the darkness.

"You know when I was in school, there was a terrible fire in this section of the theater. They rebuilt the whole thing," Mr. Cunningham says.

"I know," Cole responds, having just talked to one of the victims of the tragedy.

Onstage, Cole is the main character of the performance, playing a stable boy who is the only one to retrieve a "sword in the stone." He is then carried on the shoulders of his classmates. This is a huge win for Cole, who has spent his life bullied and tossed aside in his elementary school. He smiles broadly. This event paired with helping Kyra Collins gives the boy a newfound purpose, a glory that he had been craving prior to meeting Dr. Crowe. He is a new boy, sure that he can succeed and work with his power rather than against it. This turning point is a revelation and a relief for viewers, knowing that Cole can live a fulfilling life rather than just one of terror and trauma.

After the play, Crowe is smiling just as big as Cole as they talk in the hallway. Crowe says to Cole that it is now time for Cole to tell his mother about the secret.

"I'm not going to see you anymore, am I?" Cole asks Crowe.

Crowe shakes his head, "No."

The climax of Shyamalan's script for *The Sixth Sense* approaches in the second to last scene as Cole and Lynn Sear are in a car at a standstill. The traffic is horrible.

"I hope nobody got hurt," Lynn says, looking out the window to try to see the source of the bumper-to-bumper traffic.

"I'm ready to communicate with you," Cole says.

"Communicate?" Lynn responds in confusion.

"Tell you my secrets," Cole says.

He continues, saying that a lady died in the traffic and that is why they are stopped. The ghost is standing next to the window, a biker with her helmet cracked and hair "matted with rain and blood."

"Cole, you're scaring me," Lynn says.

"They scare me too sometimes," Cole responds.

He then continues to spill his secret. He can see ghosts, and now his mother knows. The veil is lifted. Cole can find just as much peace as the ghosts who haunt him. In order to convince his mother that what he is experiencing is true, he says, "Grandma says hi."

Lynn looks at her son in disbelief. He tells his mother that the deceased comes to visit him sometimes.

"She wanted me to tell you, she saw you dance," Cole says. "She said when you were little, you and her had a fight right before your dance recital. You thought she didn't come to see you dance. She did."

Lynn, baffled, starts to cry. The emotion in this scene is intense and heartbreaking, but lends to a resolution that we can find peaceful.

"She said, you came to where they buried her. Asked her a question. . . . She said the answer is 'Every day.' What did you ask?"

Lynn is sobbing. "Do I make her proud?"

The two embrace and the plot is finally settled with Cole and his mother. The boundaries that Cole had put up for eight years of his life have been lifted.

Shyamalan could have ended it there, with Cole finally telling his mother about his powers, but the filmmaker had a trick up his sleeve. In the final scene of Shyamalan's screenplay, we finally have a resolution for Crowe that would shock the pants off of everyone viewing the film. The final twist of *The Sixth Sense* shot Shyamalan into stardom, leading to him being compared to Steven Spielberg and Alfred Hitchcock.

Dr. Malcolm Crowe is dead. He has been dead the whole time. He died the night that Vincent Gray shot him. He was never alive. The whole time, the viewer was sure that he was the living protagonist of the film.

Crowe gets home and sees Anna, his wife, on the couch watching their wedding video. She is talking to Crowe in her sleep, saying, "I miss you. Why, Malcolm?"

"What, Anna? What did I do? What's made you so sad?" Crowe responds.

Anna says that he left her, which leaves Crowe bewildered.

Suddenly, his wedding band falls from Anna's hands and rolls on the floor. Crowe looks at his own hand and realizes his ring is gone.

He is filled with confusion. He goes to the door of his basement office, where he had spent so much time while he was alive, to see a dead bolt blocking access.

"Malcolm doesn't know what the hell's going on. . . . His eyes are drawn to the dining table. . . . Only one place setting is out on the tabletop," Shyamalan writes.

Crowe now realizes that he is dead. He places his hand on his stomach and there is blood streaming from under his shirt. The initial scene, with Malcolm and Anna in the bedroom where Malcolm was shot, plays over again, showing the viewer what really happened, showing them that he had died.

Upon this realization, Crowe is now faced with the reality that it is time for him to move into the afterlife, just as Cole's other ghosts had to accomplish in order to find true peace. Crowe backs away from his wife, tense music ensues, and Crowe tells Anna that she was never the second priority in his life. This statement tells the viewer that he is ready now to cross over. Shyamalan's script ends with Crowe watching the rest of the wedding video, professing his love for her on camera. The memories are there. The life with his wife was real. The love was there for decades. Upon sharing that last sentiment with his wife, he feels he is ready to cross over.

Shyamalan's script, with detailed notes, gruesome scenes, tender moments, and ultimately, the indication that peace can be found after we die, makes *The Sixth Sense* a horror drama to stand the test of time.

2

Selling the Thriller

At age twenty-nine, Shyamalan knew what he wanted and was determined to get it. He was confident in his worth, and even if his first two films didn't perform well at the box office, he had a feeling that his next pic would blow everyone away. Around the same age as Hitchcock when he wrote his first big film, this young filmmaker, known as Night, wanted to get out to LA and sell his screenplay for *The Sixth Sense* for $1 million dollars; otherwise, he'd shelve it. He would approach studios with an ultimatum: sell for one million bones or fuck off. Oh, and he would have to be attached as director. No exceptions. It was the kind of confidence that would result in a historic bidding war between many studios who thought, "Hey, this kid is something special."

"I have to be attached as director, and we're going to have a $1 million minimum bid," he told the *Hollywood Reporter* in 2019 of his interactions with studios while selling *The Sixth Sense*. "If they want to read it, they have to know that this is going to start at $1 million."

So, Night kissed his wife and young daughter farewell and caught a plane to LA, where he would stay at an upscale Four Seasons that was "too expensive" according to an interview with the *Hollywood Reporter* in 2019.

"I remember feeling, like, a gulp as I paid for the room. I was like, 'Well, if it doesn't sell, I guess I will really be pissed I spent whatever it was for this room.'"

As it turns out, Night would have no need to worry. Hungry studios around LA would devour *The Sixth Sense* script, recognizing the potential that the eerie storyline would have. New Line Cinema, Disney's now defunct Hollywood Pictures, Columbia Pictures, and DreamWorks would all be involved in the bidding war that would last days. Shyamalan had told his agent that he would only sell if the minimum bid was $1 million, so sure that this pic would be worth it for the major studios in Hollywood.

"I was twenty-five when I wrote [*The Sixth Sense*]. I felt that sometimes when you are writing something that no one's asked you to write, you have to decide its worth and decide how it's going to be in a kind of very specific way," Shyamalan told the *Hollywood Reporter*. "I said to my agent at the time, 'It's fine if no one wants to pay that money for it. We're not making it. If they don't want to make it, I will shelve it.' You have to not be bluffing when you say stuff like that. I wasn't bluffing. I'll do other things, but I won't make the movie."

Over the course of a few days, Shyamalan would wait for feedback and hope for bids, eager to move forward with the picture. The studios would eventually come forward with offers, but, of course, only one studio could really make the pic. And that studio would be Disney's Hollywood Pictures.

"I went over to a studio and then there was another call and they said, 'Someone else just bid, you go drive over to another studio,'" Shyalaman told the *Hollywood Reporter*. "I remember it ended with Disney hearing that another company was going to come in with a big offer. So, they called immediately and said, 'We want to close it, right now.'"

Close it they did, in a big way. In a shock to everyone in the City of Angels, Hollywood Pictures bought the pic for $2.25 million, the most aggressive deal in recent memory. Not only did the freshly appointed President David Vogel agree to the script, he also agreed to a budget of $15 million for the film.

The *Hollywood Reporter* wrote in September 1997:

> Hollywood Pictures has paid $2.25 million for M. Night Shyamalan's *The Sixth Sense*, giving Shyamalan a green light to make the film. It is one of the largest and most startling spec script sales in recent history. That payment will cover Shyamalan's writing and directing services. It could go higher and top $3 million if various bonuses kick in. Shyamalan also gets a hefty back end. Hollywood Pictures' purchase of the screenplay capped an intense flurry of bidding that started Monday afternoon and continued well into the evening before new Hollywood president David Vogel committed to buy the script. But that wasn't all he committed to. In a deal that had executives and agents all over town talking, the Disney division agreed to green light the picture, with a budget of about $15 million. That will consist of some $10 million for below-the-line costs and cast, with the other $5 million for writing, producing and directing fees.

When then-chairman of Walt Disney Pictures Joe Roth received the script, he agreed with then-president of Disney David Vogel that they needed to beat out the rest of the studios and grab hold of *The Sixth Sense*. They knew from the start that this would be a successful film and were eager to attach a huge price tag on the script. According to Roth, he said that now-disgraced Hollywood producer Harvey Weinstein called him saying that Miramax was interested in the script, but didn't want Night to direct it because he was a rookie. Fortunately for Night, Roth brushed Weinstein off and instead worked with Vogel to secure the rights to the script.

Roth recalled:

> The guy who was the president of Disney Pictures division who worked for me was named David Vogel. He read the script and he was very excited. And then I read the script and was even

more excited and basically said, "We have to buy this. We have to make sure we get it and nobody else does." . . . We did get it. And at that point they also told me that Night would be the director. I had seen the one movie Night had done and I got a phone call from Harvey Weinstein, part of my job was to supervise the Miramax account. What I didn't know was that Miramax had an option for Night to do another movie. When Harvey knew Night was going to direct it, he was very against it. I wasn't sure if it was about talent or simply about him losing his option, but I ended up saying, "Okay, [Night's] going to direct it and it's going to be for Disney. It's going to be a low budget film and I'm not going to worry about it because it's a great script."

As Disney signed on under David Vogel's leadership, well-known producers Kathleen Kennedy and Frank Marshall jumped on the wagon, and soon, international superstar Bruce Willis would be attached in the lead role as Dr. Malcolm Crowe in *The Sixth Sense*. At the time, Willis cost $20 million per film, and with only a $15 million budget for the film so far, Disney decided that they would need help with the funding. In comes Spyglass Entertainment, a brand-spanking-new company headed by Gary Barber and Roger Birnbaum. Disney's Joe Roth, along with Vogel, would approach the production and distribution outlet to see if they might be interested in making *The Sixth Sense* their first financial endeavor.

"I had told Spyglass that I would have them do five movies and *The Sixth Sense* was one of those movies," Roth said.

Co-financing partnerships like this one help save the studios from incurring losses at the box office. The more the better so that Disney alone wouldn't take a massive hit if, God forbid, *The Sixth Sense* ended up flopping. Having said that, if *The Sixth Sense* were to hit gold in multiplexes, Disney would lose out on a major chunk of profit, as they share ties with Spyglass. The deal, however, is seen as a "win-win" by Disney chairman Joe Roth. Spyglass not only agreed to help finance *The Sixth Sense*, but also was "structured to protect Disney's downside by reducing its capital investment in a slate of 15 movies over five years while giving the studio key distribution rights around the world."

Spyglass and Disney would retain a healthy working relationship beyond Night's psychological drama, protecting Disney from incurring major losses, but instead, sitting down to break bread on dozens of movies moving forward in hopes to reap major rewards. Other Spyglass/Disney movies would include *Bruce Almighty*, *Stick It*, *Eight Below*, and *The Pacifier*, mostly under-the-radar films that wouldn't necessarily live up to *The Sixth Sense* in popularity, but would instead become comedic family favorites of the 2000s.

"This is a win-win for everybody," Roth said. "The net effect is we end up with what I imagine will be $80 million to $100 million in profit [for *The Sixth Sense*]. It helped get Spyglass started and we now have a legitimate supplier that will pay for the budgets of a third of our non-Disney movies over the course of a year."

Looking back on this decision, Roth has a different opinion. If he had known how well the movie would perform, he would not have co-financed the picture. He and Disney would have produced it alone, reaping all of the benefits and not having to share a piece of the pie with anyone else.

"Would I do it again, knowing how it turned out? No, I would have not co-financed it. But again, you can see going in with a rookie director, you would try to cover your downside. Hindsight is 2020."

Spyglass would pay for the entire production costs of *The Sixth Sense*, with Birnbaum and Barber believing that the pic would succeed at the box office in overseas countries because Willis was attached.

After Birnbaum and Barber saw dailies, they were sure that Shyalaman was the next big thing, a hardworking director who knows what he wants out of his picture and each scene.

"With Bruce being in this movie, we felt we had a really good shot at not only doing well here but doing well overseas with it," Birnbaum told the *Hollywood Reporter* in August 1999. "Of course, it was in the capable hands of Frank [Marshall] and Kathy [Kennedy], which gave Gary [Barber] and I a lot of security that it would be produced well. And Barry Mendel, who had worked with Night over the years [on *Unbreakable* and *The Happening*,] assured us that he was a talent to be reckoned with. With every passing day that we saw dailies, we realized that this young film director was very, very talented."

Husband–wife team Frank Marshall and Kathleen Kennedy started their own production company, Amblin Entertainment, with Steven Spielberg in the early 1980s. The couple worked together on films such as *Raiders of the Lost Ark*, *Arachnophobia*, *Who Framed Roger Rabbit?*, *Alive*, *Congo*, and countless more. Over the course of his career, Marshall has been nominated for five Oscars for his work on *The Sixth Sense*, *The Curious Case of Benjamin Button*, *Seabiscuit*, *The Color Purple*, and *Raiders of the Lost Ark*. Kennedy would work with directors such as Spielberg, Martin Scorsese, Robert Zemeckis, Barry Levinson, and Clint Eastwood in the 1990s. She would later start an ongoing professional relationship with George Lucas, eventually stepping down from the Kennedy/Marshall production company with her spouse to take a co-chair gig at Lucasfilm Ltd. with Lucas, where she now works.

And then, there was the issue of MPAA rating and release date. When Birnbaum and Barber first read the script, they were sure that it was more of an adult film and should have an R rating. However, when the film was done, the producers believed that with Haley Joel Osment being such a young protagonist and without too many gory scenes, sexual content, or foul language from the cast members, they might be able to slap a PG-13 rating on it, accessing a younger demographic. Shyamalan would continue with this strategy for the majority of his films. His movies, such as *Devil*, *The Village*, and *Split*, along with *The Sixth Sense*, were much less gory and crass in comparison to later horror thrillers such as the *Saw* and *Hostel* franchises, which were inevitably hit with an R rating. Other, more psychological thrillers such as the John Cusack/Ray Liotta film *Identity* in 2003 and the mind-bending albeit totally confusing *Memento* in 2000 were also R-rated as they contained mature dialogue, violence, and sexual sequences. *The Sixth Sense* would pave the way for other horror thrillers/psychological dramas to be labeled PG-13, like the ghostly Nicole Kidman film *The Others* in 2001, *The Skeleton Key* with Kate Hudson in 2005, and Jim Carrey's *The Number 23* in 2007. All of those movies had twisty-turny plotlines along with big-name actors and actresses playing the lead roles.

For instance, *The Others*, set in World War II wartime 1945, stars Nicole Kidman as Grace Stewart who is a mother to children she claims are photosensitive. An elderly couple and their mute daughter show up at Stewart's door, saying that they'd love to help her care for the house. Stewart and her two children start seeing ghosts around the house. The film follows the family through paranormal occurrences until the twist happens toward the end of the movie. Like Dr. Malcolm Crowe in *The Sixth Sense*, Stewart, her children, and the elderly couple are actually dead the whole time and are the ones doing the haunting. The similarity to the twist in *The Sixth Sense* is uncanny.

"When the movie itself ends, it's on a note of ambiguity. The house will be sold again, but there's no telling how Grace and the children will cope with it now that they know they're ghosts. All we know is that they're determined to stay: 'No one can make us leave,' Grace says, sealing her family's fate as the very 'others' of a thousand haunted house stories," writes Leo Noboru Limu for *The Looper* in 2021.

Like *The Sixth Sense*, the crew of *The Others* also decided to go with a PG-13 rating, another striking similarity to Shyamalan's blockbuster hit.

"Gary [Barber] and I feel very strongly that an R rating on a movie really does put handcuffs on distribution. It really can hurt you," Birnbaum told the *Hollywood Reporter* in 1999. "Some movies demand to be R, and they can't really work if they're not. This particular picture could have easily been an R-rated movie, but we all felt it was the wise move to make it a PG-13.

"When we first read the script, it's probably safe to say we both felt this was more of an adult film. When we saw it completed, we had a feeling this movie might possibly play younger. When we got a PG-13 rating, we were very glad, but still we were not sure whether the movie was going to be a movie that younger audiences wanted to see."

Thankfully, *The Sixth Sense* would play well to younger demographics when the trailer was released. Osment, a preteen at the time, was the face of the movie more than Willis, gearing it to a younger audience who would hopefully identify with the child who suffers from social anxiety. It would play to the young outcasts of the world as they see Osment onscreen grappling with his mental afflictions and clairvoyant abilities. Yes, Willis is a big name, but the real draw of *The Sixth Sense* was Osment. Luckily, the trailer played well and the head honchos behind the flick were satisfied and eager for the film's August 1999 release.

"It wasn't [clear] until the Disney marketing team (under president Chris Pula) put together the materials. The trailer got into the marketplace and, lo and behold, we got a lot of positive reaction from all four demographic groups (younger and older males and younger and older females)," Birnbaum told the *Hollywood Reporter*.

"We realized that because we had a PG-13 rating, we would be able to capitalize on their interest. If we had an R rating, I don't think we would have been the success that we are today."

The other debate that producers tackled was when to release the picture. At first, the film was set to hit movie theaters September

10, 1999. If it had been released then, the Shyamalan original film would have had to contend with *Stigmata*, a supernatural horror film with Patricia Arquette, Gabriel Byrne, Jonathan Pryce, Nia Long, and Portia de Rossi. It would have beaten out the underground hit with no question, but instead, Birnbaum, Barber, Disney executives, and the rest of the production team decided that they would try to release it in the summertime, hoping to become the summer sleeper hit of the season.

Moving the date back to Shyalaman's birthday on August 6 was a risk that ended up being a great decision. The only real threat that weekend was *The Thomas Crown Affair* with Faye Dunaway, Pierce Brosnan, Rene Russo, and Denis Leary, which would later be nominated for its music at both the Academy Awards and the Emmys.

"Originally a fall entry, Disney sensibly moved 'Sixth Sense' into summer and used favorable reviews and creepy TV spots to effectively muscle its way into first place, with an opening weekend estimated at $25.8 million in 2,161 theaters, almost $12,000 a theater. That's the biggest August debut ever, supplanting 1993's 'The Fugitive,'" Richard Natale wrote in the *Los Angeles Times* on August 9, 1999.

"The movie was supposed to come out in October and after seeing the movie and seeing what it could be, we all agreed that we should finish it quickly and have the movie come out in August," Roth said. "It's the summer. October has never been a great playing time. It was kind of the perfect situation. We got the star [Bruce Willis]. Night turned out to be incredibly outfitted and we moved the date up to be a much more competitive date."

Meanwhile, Shyamalan was elated and relieved that his film was a success, telling Claudia Eller at the *Los Angeles Times* in 1999 that Disney's bid of $2.5 million for his script and $500,000 to direct was "absolutely historic, unprecedented. And they asked for no rewrites."

In the first few weekends at the box office, *The Sixth Sense* broke records, becoming the biggest August debut ever and then continuing to dominate until it surpassed Steven Spielberg's *Jaws* which grossed $260 million in 1975. Shyamalan, roughly the same age as Spielberg by the time *The Sixth Sense* was released, was "thrilled" when Buena Vista Pictures Distribution President Chuck Viane called him with the news. The young director told Viane that he had a poster of *Jaws* behind his desk and was a huge fan of the film and Spielberg as a director.

"Jaws had been one of those iconic films that [Shyamalan] always looked up to," Viane told the *Hollywood Reporter* in 1999. "It's just one of those calls you love to make."

The Sixth Sense, according to Roth and countless others, was revolutionary for the horror-drama genre and made Shyamalan a household name. The rookie director knew that he had something truly special and stopped at nothing to get the film made. His tenacity, dedication, and perseverance led to a historical bidding war between multiple Hollywood studios, ending with Disney's Hollywood Pictures securing the script and Night as director. Everyone knew *The Sixth Sense* was something special even if they didn't realize then just how monumental the success would be. According to Roth, the making of *The Sixth Sense* was great from start to finish.

3

Building the Cast

Once Shyalaman sold the movie to Disney's Hollywood Pictures, it was time to put a cast together. Shyamalan worked with Avy Kaufman, an industry bigwig known for her work on *Succession*, *Brokeback Mountain*, *National Treasure*, and Shyamalan's *Wide Awake*, to build a cast that would be perfect for the horror drama. Avy would meet with cast members such as Mischa Barton to secure the roles in *The Sixth Sense*.

They would need a stern yet soft-sided Dr. Malcolm Crowe. They would need a young boy who could deliver his lines with a mix of innocence and fear for Cole Sear. For the part of Lynn Sear, Shyamalan would need a strong female figure to play a single mother concerned for her son's mental and physical health while being unaware that her son could see the dead. Vincent Gray, the estranged patient, would need to be played by someone who could dedicate themselves to playing a mentally unstable patient to deeply disturb the viewer. Dr. Crowe's wife would need to be someone graceful and introverted, docile and kind. Kyra Collins, the young girl who fell victim to her mother's Munchausen by proxy diagnosis, would need to be similar to Osment, innocent and fearful all at once. Kaufman and Shyamalan would see many actors throughout their process, and some of them were knockouts immediately.

Haley Joel Osment was blown away by the script and Shyamalan knew he was his Cole Sear the second he started reading for the writer and director. Haley Joel was ten years old at the time and had appeared in *Forrest Gump*, playing Tom Hanks's son. He had also appeared in network sitcoms and dramas such as *The Jeff Foxworthy Show*, *Murphy Brown*, *Ally McBeal*, *Walker: Texas Ranger*, and *Thunder Alley*, prior to working on *The Sixth Sense*.

"I'd never read a script like [*The Sixth Sense*]. I had done some films, and I had some network sitcoms. This script was a whole other ball game," Osment said. "In terms of the whole process starting with the audition, it was kind of the first time at around age 10 that I think I started to get a real understanding of what acting was and everything and getting used to being on sets, learning your lines and the job part of it."

When Osment first read the script, he had nightmares from Shyamalan's writing. When he and his father went to audition, Osment was not thinking of himself as an actor wanting the part, but rather going in as Cole Sear himself, a sensitive boy going about his life, able to see the dead.

"I went in there not thinking about Haley Osment wanting the role, I thought about Cole Sear going in to live, just to do something normal for him," Osment told *Good Morning America* in 1999. "When my dad and I got in the car to go down to Santa Monica to audition, I got in the car and on the way down there I was just thinking that 'you're the character, you're the character, you're Cole Sear, you're him.' You put aside anything that happened that day, you forget about Haley Osment, and you go down there and be the character."

Osment's dedication to the character of Cole Sear, his look as an innocent young ten-year-old, and his growing repertoire, made him a shoo-in for Shyamalan the second that he started reading his scenes. In an interview with Bobbie Wygant, Osment said he read three scenes for Shyamalan for his audition for the role of Cole Sear.

"My dad and I, after reading the script, we both liked it a lot. After we got the three scenes, we rehearsed them for a long time at home. My father's an actor," Osment told Wygant in 1999. "By the time we auditioned it, we had also read the script over and we just learned as much as we could about Cole, how to become him, what he was about. After auditioning for it, we just knew Cole so well that it was good."

Osment went on to tell Wygant that he can cry on cue and did so during his audition, take after take. Reading the script multiple times, he got used to the heavy content and became more and more comfortable playing the troubled young boy.

"When Haley came in and read, I knew he was the kid the second he read it. I felt overwhelmed with that knowledge," Shyamalan said of Osment's audition.

According to an interview in *Esquire* magazine, actor Michael Cera read for the role of Cole Sear, but did not get the part. He read the scene where Dr. Crowe does a magic trick with a penny, and instead of reading it as a sad boy, he read it as upbeat, perhaps leading to his rejection of the role as Cole Sear.

"I auditioned for 'The Sixth Sense,' which I didn't know was about seeing dead people. They didn't mention that in the breakdown," Cera told *Esquire* in 2009. "It's a very emotional scene. And I did not do it that way. I did it upbeat. I said 'Some magic's real' very optimistically. There is this strange sense of competition among child actors. There were a few kids, I knew if I saw them at the audition, they were going to get the part."

Bruce Willis, already known for his work in *Pulp Fiction, Die Hard*, and *The Fifth Element*, started what would become a friendship and ongoing working relationship with Shyamalan with his casting of Dr. Malcolm Crowe in *The Sixth Sense*. In an interview with ex-chairman of Disney Joe Roth, he recalled receiving a call from Willis's agent, Arnold Rifkin, saying that Willis was interested in the part of Dr. Malcolm Crowe in *The Sixth Sense*, but the agent wouldn't let Willis sign on with Night directing. Roth said that it is common for agents to reject material helmed by rookie filmmakers, but luckily, Roth and president of Disney David Vogel convinced Willis to at least meet with the young Night, and he agreed.

Roth recalled:

> So, I speak to Rifkin and he says Bruce Willis wants to [play Dr. Crowe,] but he's not going to do it with Shyamalan being director. I said, "Well, then, he's not going to do the movie." And then, Arnold agreed to have Bruce meet Night. Night was a young guy and this was going to be a big meeting, and he was nervous about it. He was a kid at that point, he wasn't the same guy he is now. I called Night up and I said, "You're going to have a meeting with Bruce Willis. It's going to be fine because you're the writer of this script, so you can answer any questions that he would have." The meeting went great. Bruce was going to do the movie with Night. So now, it becomes a slightly bigger movie with a movie star in it.

That meeting would be the start of an ongoing professional relationship between Willis and Night. Willis would later appear in Shyamalan's film *Unbreakable* as superhuman David Dunn. Two decades later, he would reprise the role for *Glass*, released in 2019. Willis's tough guy exterior in many of his roles is balanced with a sense of empathy and calm which he carries effortlessly in *The Sixth Sense* as well, making him an ideal child psychologist for the film.

Willis's career had already begun when he teamed up with Shyamalan for *The Sixth Sense*. Born Walter Bruce Willis in 1955 in a West Germany town called Idar-Oberstein, the young aspiring actor moved to New Jersey with his family in 1957. His mother, Marlene, is German and his father is an American who went to Germany to serve in the army. He would later become the eldest of four Willis children. He has a brother named David, a sister named Florence, and a second brother named Robert who died from cancer in 2001. While in New Jersey, his father worked as a welder, a mechanic, and a factory worker while his mother, Marlene, worked at a bank.

When Willis was young, his parents divorced. He went on to live with his father while the other three children went to live with their mother. In school, Willis said that he found a love for reading, but struggled with a severe stutter which made him particularly insecure. He did well in school and would audition for a school play called *A Connecticut Yankee in King Arthur's Court*. Upon getting a part in the play, he realized that he didn't stutter when he was on stage. Soon, he was auditioning and performing in theater as a high school kid, which made him more confident and popular with the other kids in school.

"When I acted, I was being a different person," Willis told David Sheff of *Playboy* in 1996. "The emotional trigger that caused me to stutter—I don't know what the fuck it was—stopped when I would act. Finally, I told myself I wasn't going to be affected by it and I grew out of it."

During high school, Willis was expelled for a physical fight with another student, and when he was nineteen, he was arrested for possession of marijuana after donning two joints in public, one behind each ear. After getting kicked out of school, he worked as a security guard at the Salem nuclear power plant in New Jersey, a bus driver for the Dupont chemical company, and also took a crack at studying to be a private detective. Nothing hit his soul quite like acting on a stage, and soon, the twentysomething was back on the path to becoming one of the biggest actors Hollywood has ever seen.

He studied theater at Montclair State College, but was never patient enough to take classes on the subject. He just wanted to be where the action was, without having to sit in a classroom. He spent a year at Montclair before dropping out and moving to New York

City to star in Off-Broadway productions and television commercials. While in school, he would cut class to go door to door introducing himself to Broadway theater attendants, but nothing took for quite some time. Finally, he got a role in an Off-Broadway play when he was twenty-two years old, and after securing this job, he officially dropped out of Montclair.

While working on-stage, Willis had to make some extra money, so he started working as a bartender and waiter at restaurants and bars across Manhattan. He worked at Centrale, a bar where Broadway actors would regularly stop in to wind down after long days rehearsing and performing. He started acting in episodic roles and commercials. The first time he was on screen was in the 1980 film *The First Deadly Sin*, where he can be seen for just a split second entering a restaurant in a cap. Two years later, Willis was seen in the 1982 Paul Newman film *The Verdict*, where he played an observer in the court. In 1984, Levi's hired Willis to participate in a commercial. He is only in it for a couple of seconds, dancing in jeans on the street, but in an interview with *Playboy*, he said that he made some good "dough" on the project. In the mid-1980s, Willis also participated in the television series for *Miami Vice*, where he played Tony Amatio, a rough-and-tumble international arms dealer.

His first big gig was starring opposite Cybill Shepherd in the television sitcom *Moonlighting* in the 1980s. He almost didn't get the part. A representative for ABC thought that Willis just was not right for the part of a detective as he had a pierced ear and a disheveled, almost punk rock haircut. Luckily, the creator of *Moonlighting*, Glenn Gordon Caron, saw something special in the unknown actor and brought him in to audition opposite Shepherd. Apparently, there were at least 3,000 other people who wanted to play Willis's part. He beat them all. *Moonlighting* would go on to be nominated for sixteen Emmy Awards, including Best Actor for Willis.

"[*Moonlighting*] definitely turned out to be bigger than what I had imagined, but I knew it was good when I saw early scenes," Willis told *Playboy*.

By the end of the third season, ratings for the ABC show started to decline. Willis started to lose interest and Sheperd was also pregnant. Willis started taking on movie roles, one being a romantic comedy called *Blind Date*, with Kim Basinger, directed by Blake Edwards in 1987. In the film, Willis plays Walter Davis, a jokester who doesn't really take life or romance seriously. He continued to work on commercials, too, appearing opposite Sharon Stone for Seagram's in the later 1980s. The 1980s were truly busy for Willis as he also released a blues/soul album called *The Return of Bruno*, which would go on to make fourteenth place on the Billboard 200 list, a single, "Respect Yourself," scored fifth place on the American charts.

Upon leaving *Moonlighting*, Willis was offered a huge film which would put him on the map as an actor to watch: *Die Hard*. Sylvester Stallone, Richard Gere, Harrison Ford, and Arnold Schwarzenegger were Willis's competition, but for various reasons, all but him turned down the role. Willis was offered a whopping $5 million for the part of John McClane, a fee that, to Alan Ladd Jr., then MGM chairman, would "throw the whole movie business out of whack." When Willis signed on, the script was rewritten with him in mind, turning the character from a savagely cruel ball-buster into more of a comedic hero. Willis's McClane is a sarcastic, stereotypical New Yorker who works to free hostages from a terrorist organization in a hotel he is staying in. After the first *Die Hard* film, he went on to make *Die Hard 2* (1990), *Die Hard with a Vengeance* (1995), *Live Free or Die Hard* (2007), and *A Good Day to Die Hard* (2013).

Willis took on a lesser-known Blake Edwards movie titled *Sunset*, released in 1988 opposite James Garner and Malcolm McDowell. The film was a western mystery that did not perform well at the box office. In 1989, a year later and just after *Die Hard*, Willis starred in Norman Jewison's *In Country*, a drama in which Willis plays the main character's uncle, Emmett Smith, who, as a Vietnam vet, is traumatized by memories of the war. His niece, played by Emily Lloyd, lives with him and tries to get information about her late father, who was killed in Vietnam before she was born. The portrayal of Emmett Smith earned Willis a Golden Globe nomination even though the picture did not perform well at the box office.

And then, there was Willis's first film with John Travolta, whom he would work with again in *Pulp Fiction* a few years later. Willis voiced a toddler protagonist in director Amy Heckerling's romantic comedy *Look Who's Talking* about a single mother (played by Kirstie Alley) who gives birth to the son of a married man and then finds a new romantic partner in James (played by Travolta). The talking child protagonist, much like later movies such as *Baby Geniuses* in 1999 and the animated *Boss Baby* in 2017, are undoubtedly as creepy as they are hilarious, and *Look Who's Talking* made significant waves at the box office, grossing $297 million.

For the next few years in the early 1990s, Willis starred in a series of flops and cult hits. Some, he agreed, like the 1990 comedy *The Bonfire of the Vanities* opposite Tom Hanks and Melanie Griffith, directed by Brian De Palma, were commercial flops. He said in an interview with *Playboy* that he would "not do it again," referring to the disaster that was *The Bonfire of the Vanities*.

"I was miscast. I know that Tom Hanks thinks he was, too," Willis told *Playboy*. "The movie was based on a great book. But one problem with the story, when it came to the film, was that there was no one in it you could root for. In most successful movies, there's someone to cheer on."

Hudson Hawk was one of those films that was later hailed as a "cult hit." Michael Lehmann's *Hudson Hawk* was released in 1991 and followed Hawk, played by Willis, who is a criminal mastermind recently released from prison. The story follows the thief as he believes he is being blackmailed into robbing the Vatican by the CIA. The comedic/action thriller grossed $97 million at the box office and succeeded as well on home video, raking in mixed reviews. Roger Ebert and *Variety* agreed that the film was silly and unsuccessful, but in this case, Willis disagreed with the critics.

"If [critics] put their mind to it, they can crush a movie or an actor. The critical media in general can conspire to make people feel fucking stupid if they see a movie. It happened with 'Hudson Hawk.' It had nothing to do with the film," Willis told *Playboy*. "After the criticism I received for 'Hudson Hawk,' I stood back and looked at how much power I was giving to these people. I thought, If they say I'm good, am I good? If they say I suck, do I suck? I realized that wasn't the scale by which to measure oneself."

Two more films were released with Willis attached in the same year as *Hudson Hawk* and they were more positively received in the press. These included *The Last Boy Scout* and *Mortal Thoughts*, with Willis's then wife/actress Demi Moore. *The Last Boy Scout* faced difficulties during production with constant rewrites to the script and disagreements between the writer and the studio. *Mortal Thoughts* required Willis to play a drug addict and rapist, a challenging role for someone like Willis who had been constantly playing humorous, likable characters in his filmography.

A true cult staple of Willis's career is Robert Zemeckis's *Death Becomes Her* featuring Goldie Hawn and Meryl Streep. Bruce Willis plays a drunkard and spineless husband to Goldie Hawn who leaves her for a famous actress, Madeline Ashton, played by Meryl Streep. Hawn's character, Helen Sharp, returns to her home after spending time in a psychiatric hospital to confront Ashton and Willis's character Ernest Menville. Ashton discovers that Sharp has been taking a drug to make her immortal and youthful and decides to try it herself. Menville, however, is too afraid of the repercussions to take the drug, too. The black comedy was the first to make use of CGI to change the texture of the skin and ended up grossing an impressive $149 million at the box office. *Death Becomes Her* would go on to win the Academy Award for Best Visual Effects.

In *Pulp Fiction*, released in 1994, he played professional boxer Butch Coolidge. Starring opposite John Travolta, Samuel L. Jackson, Uma Thurman, Christopher Walken, and Steve Buscemi under the direction of the legendary Quentin Tarantino gave the film enough star power to shine with a unique script written by the director. At first, Tarantino wanted to cast Sylvester Stallone for the part of Butch Coolidge because he wanted someone who already had a remarkable legacy in Hollywood, which Stallone had already succeeded in with *Rocky*. Luckily for Willis, Tarantino saw something special in him when he met the growing star at a barbecue hosted by Harvey Keitel and decided to offer the role to him.

Willis told *Playboy*:

> Harvey Keitel's little girl came over to the house one day to play with our girls. He came to get her. It was after he had done "Bad Lieutenant" and "Reservoir Dogs." I was talking with him about those movies and he said, "You know, Quentin's doing a new film. There are a lot of good parts in it. You should talk to him." I got the script that day. Harvey happened to be having a barbecue at his house the next day and I walked down and met Quentin. We talked for a long time and I told him I wanted to be in the film. The script was so good.

Butch Coolidge is an egocentric and hotheaded boxer, laying low in Los Angeles to hide from mob bosses who may be out to kill him. His sweet relationship with Fabienne (played by Maria de Medeiros) mirrors his relationship with Olivia Williams's character in *The Sixth Sense* along with his stoicism with a kind heart hidden underneath the tough guy facade.

Pulp Fiction won the Palme d'Or at the Cannes Film Festival where it shocked viewers and made a promising reputation before hitting movie theaters. It grossed over $100 million and earned seven Oscar nominations with one win awarded to Quentin Tarantino and Roger Avery for Best Screenplay.

The next two films that followed *Pulp Fiction* included a cameo role in the comedy *Four Rooms*. The film was shot by four directors: Allison Anders, Alexander Rockwell, Robert Rodriguez, and Quentin Tarantino. Willis appeared in this film for free and took his name off of the titles because according to the Screen Actors Guild rules, actors shouldn't be acting for no income.

Willis then went to play Cole in *12 Monkeys* in 1995. His character is a time traveler from the year 2035 who has knowledge of a fatal virus that kills the majority of the world's population. The sci-fi epic screams a foreshadowing of the COVID-19 pandemic. The film, ironically, just celebrated its twenty-fifth anniversary during the height of the sickness spreading across the world. Brad Pitt starred alongside Willis and was eventually nominated for his first Oscar for his performance. Many on the set of *12 Monkeys* recognized Willis bringing in what he had learned and grown accustomed to with his *Die Hard* character, a true tough guy.

"Bruce is remarkable in the movie, but for Terry (Gilliam, director) there were a lot of takes that were very, he would say, *Die Hard*. That Bruce Willis," said Madeleine Stowe to the *Hollywood Reporter* back in 2021.

Mick Audsley, editor of *12 Monkeys*, praised Willis for his acting chops while talking to the *Hollywood Reporter* for the film's twenty-fifth anniversary.

"Bruce has terrific craft skills, of getting into the right place. Repeating things, which we had done at six in the morning and then nine o'clock at night three weeks later, to be able to match it and all that stuff. He's got all of those wonderful skills that are less visible outside of the cutting room," said Ausdley. "But you get to appreciate them in my job because it reduces the work of bringing things together and making a performance shape."

12 Monkeys earned $168 million at the box office and Willis won for his work, receiving the Saturn Award for Best Actor.

And then there's *The Fifth Element*, another science-fiction action film which was released in 1997 to big box office numbers and fairly positive reviews from critics. The film, set in the twenty-third century, was directed by Luc Besson, also known for his writing on *Leon: The Professional* starring a young Natalie Portman. Willis, alongside Milla Jovovich's character Leeloo, work together to find four metaphysical stones that would help defend the Earth from an asteroid on its way to destroy the planet. The film opened the 1997 Cannes Film Festival and debuted at $17 million on opening weekend, going on to gross $263 million on a $90 million budget.

Critics were mixed in their reviews of *The Fifth Element*. Some said it was hard to follow while others praised its over-the-top nature. Kevin Thomas of the *Los Angeles Times* said it was an "elaborate, even campy sci-fi extravaganza, which is nearly as hard to follow as last year's *Mission: Impossible*" concluding that it is "a lot warmer, more fun, and boasts some of the most sophisticated, witty production and costume design you could ever hope to see."

Willis became known for choosing roles based on his own personal taste. He wouldn't just accept anything that dropped on his desk. He wanted to play characters that were unique and layered with dialogue and character development that intrigued him and piqued his interest. Films like *The Fifth Element* did not make him millions like *Die Hard* did, but because of the originality of the screenplay, he took roles like these which he thought were memorable and distinctive.

"I really choose films to satisfy myself, I don't really concern myself with what I think the audience wants," Willis told Bobbie Wygant in an interview in 1988.

And then, there's *Armageddon*. Released in 1998, a year before *The Sixth Sense* opened at the box office, the cast was stacked with stars. Willis plays Harry S. Stamper, an oil driller who, alongside other astronauts, are called to destroy an asteroid headed for Earth. He plays another tough guy and is joined by Ben Affleck, Steve Buscemi, Owen Wilson, William Fichtner, Will Patton, Michael Clarke Duncan, Liv Tyler, and Billy Bob Thornton. Critics accused Michael Bay of being inaccurate in his storytelling of astronaut launches, saying that there were technical inconsistencies in the image of the Mir orbital station and the dialogue between astronauts contained gross errors. Bay defended himself in interviews saying that the pressure to finish the movie in sixteen weeks made it impossible for Bay to give the film the time and work it needed to be successful and accurate.

"I will apologize for Armageddon, because we had to do the whole movie in 16 weeks. It was a massive undertaking. That was not fair to the movie. I would redo the entire third act if I could. But the studio literally took the movie away from us. It was terrible," Bay told the *Miami Herald* in 2013.

A year later, it was time for Willis to make waves in Shyamalan's 1999 motion picture *The Sixth Sense*. Willis's strong repertoire and ability to nail the "tough guy with a soft heart" personality made him an asset to *The Sixth Sense* cast and shot him into mega-stardom that rivaled Tom Cruise and Nicolas Cage, two other prominent actors of the 1990s.

Willis was attached to the film because of a contractual agreement with Disney in which the two affirmed that the bigshot actor would appear in two films for the studio. Slated to appear in the 1997 romantic comedy *Broadway Brawler*, that film would be shut down weeks into production, so Disney worked out a deal with Willis in which he would later appear in two Disney studio films after this one failed. One of them would be *The Sixth Sense*. David Vogel, head of

Buena Vista Motion Picture Group, sent the script to Willis's agent and the actor was "blown away." At first, Willis's agent wanted to nix Shyamalan as the director, but luckily, the agent would back off and the Indian American would continue his work on *The Sixth Sense* with Willis attached to star.

"When I read [the script for] *The Sixth Sense*, when I turned that last page, the last three pages of that script, I was blown away by the fact that my character was dead," Willis said in a 2002 interview with *Reader's Digest*. "I didn't see it coming. And that's what made me want to do it. I went, 'If we can pull this off, it would be brilliant.'"

Willis would be paid a whopping $100 million for the film. Willis is now considered one of the highest paid actors throughout his career, despite many flops and failures.

Willis also dabbled in music in the 1980s when he released his debut album, *The Return of Bruno*. Bruno Randolini was Willis's alter ego, a harmonica-slinging, bluesy, eighties-era rockstar. On the record, Willis worked with the Pointer Sisters, Billy Preston, and the Temptations to cover famous songs such as "Under the Boardwalk," "Secret Agent Man/James Bond is Back," "Respect Yourself," "Down in Hollywood," and "Fun Time." "Down in Hollywood" was originally made famous by Ry Cooder, and "Fun Time" was written by Allen Toussaint, performed by Joe Cocker.

The Return of Bruno, released in 1987, made it on the Billboard top 200, securing the fourteenth spot. The album would hold the fourth position on the UK Album Charts. Willis's "Respect Yourself" cover with the Pointer Sisters on backup would become a huge eighties hit, securing the fourth position on the Billboard Hot 100, number 7 on the UK Singles Chart, and number 8 on the Canadian RMP Top Singles Chart. Other singles such as "Under the Boardwalk," and "Young Blood," appeared on the charts, but did not see as great a success as "Respect Yourself."

An HBO special with the same name as the album was released as a kind of mockumentary following Willis's alter ego Bruno Randolini. Phil Collins, Michael J. Fox, Elton John, Jon Bon Jovi, Ringo Starr, Brian Wilson, Dick Clark, and the Bee Gees participated in the documentary, discussing how Randolini influenced their careers.

Willis would release another album, *If It Don't Kill You, It Just Makes You Stronger*, in 1989. His harmonica riffs and bluesy style make the album perfect for Motown Records, the studio that also produced his debut album. The big band music is catchy and worthy of some toe-tapping and shagging, showing off Willis's talent on the harmonica and vocally.

In 1999, Willis released his last studio album titled *Classic Bruce Willis*, featuring remastered versions of songs he had already released along with a few new hits. The album did not reach the same level of popularity as his first album, but still solidified him as not only an accomplished actor, but also a talented musician in his own right.

Over the years since Willis released his two albums, he has dabbled in live performances. In 2008, he got onstage at the *Sin City* premiere to play a cover of "Devil Woman" where he shreds the harmonica and croons with a talented backup band. He is full of star power on stage, looking comfortable, happy, and in his element.

Most recently, Willis's family released an Instagram video of Willis riffing on the harmonica with friend and fellow musician Derek Richard Thomas. The clip is shot in black and white, showing Willis sitting on a staircase playing the harmonica while Thomas strums some bluesy chords on acoustic guitar. This video comes a few months after the Willis family announced that Bruce had been battling an aphasia diagnosis for quite some time now and would need to retire from acting because of his health issues.

"To Bruce's amazing supporters, as a family we wanted to share that our beloved Bruce has been experiencing some health issues and has recently been diagnosed with aphasia, which is impacting his cognitive abilities," the Willis family wrote on Instagram. "As a result of this and with much consideration, Bruce is stepping away from the career that has meant so much to him. As Bruce always says, 'Live it up' and together we plan to do just that."

According to the *Los Angeles Times*, many who worked with Bruce over the last few years have noticed a decline in the actor's memory and cognitive abilities. On the set of *Out of Death* in 2020 with director Mike Burns, the filmmaker started picking up on Willis's inability to remember his lines and sent an email to the screenwriter, saying, "It looks like we need to knock down Bruce's page count by about 5 pages. We also need to abbreviate his dialogue a bit so that there are no monologues, etc."

Although a reason was not given at the time, many people who worked with Willis over the past few years have realized what has been happening. Those with an aphasia diagnosis have problems communicating and remembering things, making it very hard for an actor to remember and execute lines on cue. Willis would soon need an "earwig," where the actor would receive his lines from a fellow actor via an in-ear piece. He was also unable to do his action stunts, requiring a body double for those scenes.

According to the *Los Angeles Times*, there was one occasion on the set of *Hard Kill* where Willis fired a gun on set on the wrong cue. Luckily, no one was injured.

For Burns, he was conflicted upon working with the actor, and after one day of filming, he realized he would need to shorten Willis's scenes and only work with the actor for one day. Judging by how Willis was acting on set, he didn't think that the actor could work effectively on set for more than a day or so. It was a hard decision for Burns, but ultimately the director shortened Willis's screen time and only worked with him for a couple of days.

"I didn't think he was better; I thought he was worse," Burns told the *Los Angeles Times*. "After we finished, I said: 'I'm done. I'm not going to do any other Bruce Willis movies.' I am relieved that he is taking time off."

Soon, Willis's team at CAA would step in to help the actor who was suffering and declining in health. They would stipulate in contractual agreements that Willis was to only work for two days. On those days, he would only be allowed to work for eight hours, but in reality, he would only work for four hours each day.

While working on the low-budget film *White Elephant*, the director, Jesse V. Johnson, noticed that Bruce was not the same person he remembered. Concerned for his cognitive health, Johnson went to Bruce's team to ask what the deal was with his health and acting abilities.

"[Bruce's team] stated that he was happy to be there, but that it would be best if we could finish shooting him by lunch and let him go early," Johnson told the *Los Angeles Times*. According to Johnson, Willis would often not know where he was or what he was doing, which alarmed cast and crew members alike. "[He would say,] I know why you're here, and I know why you're here, but why am I here?" crew members told the *Times*.

Even though Willis was in high demand, all of those filmmakers that he worked with could see that something was clearly wrong with him. Even though their movie would succeed internationally with Bruce's name attached, many filmmakers did not think it was worth it. Bruce was suffering and everyone around him knew that it was time to move on from acting altogether.

"He just looked so lost, and he would say, 'I'll do my best.' He always tried his best," Terri Martin, the production supervisor on *White Elephant*, told the *Los Angeles Times*. "He is one of the all-time greats, and I have the utmost admiration and respect for his body of work, but it was time for him to retire."

For now, Willis is taking it easy with his family, who are by his side all the time to make sure he is comfortable and safe. It was a hard truth for everyone in Hollywood and for fans of the action star to learn, but hopefully the megastar is getting the help he needs. For Shyamalan and the rest of the cast of *The Sixth Sense*, Willis will be remembered as a Hollywood icon, able to deliver lines with depth and heart as Dr. Malcolm Crowe. For Osment, he was a role model. For Shyamalan, he was a friend, the first one to give the filmmaker a hangover and someone who would appear in many of Shyamalan's movies over the years.

Toni Collette, recognized for her work in *Muriel's Wedding* in 1994 and fresh off of *Velvet Goldmine*, a film set in the 1970s flower power movement, Collette went into her audition for the part of Lynn Sear with a shaved head. In *Velvet Goldmine*, she played the lead character's wife Mandy Slade, a firecracker partier who cheats on her husband, Brian Slade, a "past his prime" glam rocker. Collette's complicated character received rave reviews by critics after the film and would catch the eye of Willis, who vouched for her in the audition process for *The Sixth Sense*. She beat out Marisa Tomei among other female actors for the role of Lynn Sear.

Shyamalan recalls:

> I had seen *Muriel's Wedding* and Toni came in and her head was shaved, and I forget if it was for fun or if it was for a movie. She did such a beautiful job. . . . I didn't want to show the video to the studio for fear that they would be concerned with her appearance, and I said "I want to cast the woman from *Muriel's Wedding*" and then Bruce backed me and said "Oh, I love *Muriel's Wedding*," so we kind of got it without the studio seeing the audition, and I was so lucky. Toni is actually wearing a wig throughout all of *The Sixth Sense*, and I think it's a wig from *Velvet Goldmine*. We didn't even have the wig.

Colette told the *Movie Show* in 1999:

> [The script] was sent to me, my agent said, "It's a Disney film and Bruce Willis is attached." And I didn't read it. I was jet lagged and I was in New York and it was very early in the morning and I thought, "I need to read something," and I picked it up and I was hooked and I sobbed for a very long time afterwards and I was immediately connected to it. I know it's being sold as a scary movie, but it's not a gratuitous, "Boo!" situation. It's very emotionally driven and the characters are all really complex and you're interested in them. It's an original unusual story and the way it's told, the way it's shot, the trust that the director has to let shots linger and let moments live out, it's like an independent film that accidentally became commercial. It's a studio's wet dream because it's commercial and it's got certain potency.

Collette was born by the name Antonia Collette on November 1, 1972, in Sydney, New South Wales, Australia. She grew up in the Sydney suburb of Blacktown until she earned a scholarship from the Australian Theatre for Young People in 1989 when she was just seventeen years old. She then attended the National Institute of Dramatic Art and dropped out to work on her first film, *Spotswood*, (also known as *The Efficiency Report*) released in 1992. In the film, Collette plays Anthony Hopkins' love interest as his character, Errol Wallace, works as a business consultant in a moccasin factory called Balls. Russell Crowe stars opposite Collette (Wendy Robinson) as a salesman for Balls. The film earned a 62 percent rating on Rotten Tomatoes and earned a small $179,469 worldwide.

The young actor delved into theatre with an appearance as Sonya in Anton Chekov's *Uncle Vanya* at the Sydney Theater in 1992. The play follows a family working to get their son-in-law off his feet after his wife dies. Collette plays the protagonist Professor Serebryakov's daughter who grows envious of her father's new, younger, more attractive wife, Yelena.

And then, there's *Muriel's Wedding* and *Velvet Goldmine*. In *Muriel's Wedding*, filmmaker P. J. Hogan told *Variety* that it is a movie about "self-esteem" as the awkward Muriel Heslop (played by Collette and based on Hogan's sister) tries to find love by embezzling money from her family to go on a trip to find her significant other. Colette decided to gain over forty pounds for the role, which she told Bobbie Wygant in 1995 was necessary as her weight was a physical extension of how she feels uncomfortable and insecure in herself. At the time, she was working with a dietician to gain weight in the safest way possible. She told Wygant that she didn't actually realize what an undertaking gaining that much weight was until she decided to lose it all after the role.

"I think most people feel like an awkward outsider at some point in their lives," Collette told *Variety's* Susan King in an email interview for the twenty-fifth anniversary of the film. "It's a part of being human. Insecurity amongst other hurdles exists to be overcome. I am realizing audiences were generally comforted by Muriel. It still makes them feel less alone and okay about feeling vulnerable and imperfect in a society that demands so much of us."

Upon auditioning for the role, Collette knew she had the part. She could feel it deep in her core, according to the Susan King interview for *Variety*.

"The whole experience seemed predestined," said Collette, "I waited three months to hear that I had the part but I was quietly confident during that period."

Rachel Griffiths, who starred opposite Collette, believed that the film was "ahead of its time" by including a "flawed heroine." This three-dimensional, authentic role is what would eventually shoot Collette into the limelight and prepare her for her role in *Velvet Goldmine*, which was released just a year before *The Sixth Sense*.

Velvet Goldmine was not very well-received when it came out in 1998. In an interview with Index Magazine in 2003, Collette recalls working with filmmaker Todd Haynes (known for his later work on *Carol* and *I'm Not There*), who was unfazed by the response.

"Todd's one of those directors that doesn't give a shit about how his films are received. He's simply telling the story that he needs to tell," Collette told interviewer Ariana Speyer. "Because he wrote the script and his vision was so clear, he was really able to influence my performance."

Collette, constantly covered in glitter and embracing the seventies era, enjoyed working with the director even if the movie was not well-received, earning $1,053,788 worldwide and a 59 percent rating on Rotten Tomatoes.

Collette's rise to stardom hit a high note in *The Sixth Sense*, when she was nominated for the Academy Award for Best Supporting Actress. After the film, she acted in pictures such as *About a Boy* alongside Hugh Grant and a young Nicholas Hoult, *In Her Shoes* with Cameron Diaz, and *Little Miss Sunshine* with Steve Carell and Abigail Breslin. Her portrayals of complicated mother figures, including her more recent roles in *Hereditary*, *Pieces of Her*, and *Knives Out*, make her stand out as an Oscar-worthy actor capable of delving into memorable, complex female characters.

When Donnie Wahlberg auditioned for *The Sixth Sense*, he came in unbathed and after a considerable amount of weight loss. He had sifted through the script on a plane in 1998 and cried when he read it. He didn't think that the part of Gray fit him. First of all, the man was too young. Second, he was not physically fit, in fact, he was emaciated.

"Nothing about me was right for the part, except for my total enthusiasm for the script," said Wahlberg.

Wahlberg decided to meet Shyamalan regardless of what he thought. Shyamalan met with him and decided that a workable age for Gray would be twenty years old. Wahlberg, twenty-eight at the time, could still conceivably pass as a twenty-year-old, in Shyamalan's eyes.

Six months after their first meeting, Wahlberg went back and Shyamalan offered him the part. The fee given to Wahlberg for his day of filming was much too low, according to his agent, but the young Wahlberg didn't care.

"I said, 'I don't care, I'd do it for free,'" Wahlberg told *USA Today*. "So I took the part and I subsequently fired my manager for telling me to pass."

Known for performing in the boyband New Kids on the Block, he is unrecognizable as the role of Vincent Gray, an estranged patient of Dr. Malcolm Crowe. Shirtless, pants-less Wahlberg appeared in the first scene of the film and set the horror in motion, shooting and killing Dr. Crowe.

"And then, of course, there was Donnie [Wahlberg], who was kind of a lightning bolt for us," Shyamalan said. "And, again, he, like Haley, brought a serious kind of commitment to his role, and even though it was one scene, he really, really lived in it, he lost tons of weight and didn't bathe. He really went for it, and it comes off."

During the first table read, Wahlberg had the idea that he would be naked during his scene at the start of the movie, and soon, everyone would be on board to have Wahlberg in just his tighty-whities. He would also lose over forty pounds for the role, showing up to set at 139 pounds. He was so unrecognizable that Night passed him on set without even knowing who he was. Wahlberg told *USA Today* that he was hungry and depressed.

"I would fast for a couple of days at a time and then just eat vegetables, chew gum all day and then walk the streets," Wahlberg told the *Hollywood Reporter* in 2019. "When I got to Philadelphia, I slept in the park one night and was going through this really crazy process."

During his day of filming, Wahlberg fell to the floor in tears, shocking the rest of the cast and crew.

"I fell on the floor, and I remember Bruce was like, 'Whoa!' and I was bawling my eyes out. M. Night came running over and was hugging me. He was like, 'That was so unbelievable.' I was thinking that I'm done. And M. Night was like, 'Okay. Can you do it again?' I was like, 'What?' I thought I had to nail it in one shot," says Wahlberg. "But I had, like, eight hours of work ahead of me."

Wahlberg's acting career was then set in motion, appearing in the television mini-series *Band of Brothers*, the *Saw* franchise, and *Blue Bloods*, which ran from 2010 to present day.

"[*The Sixth Sense*] was a game-changer for me. Every day for years people would say, 'Dude, I didn't know *that* was you,'" Wahlberg told *USA Today* in 2019. "At that time, I did exactly what I needed to do for the role. I had to look like I was going through hell. I went to a really dark place."

Mischa Barton, who played Kyra Collins, a ghost girl who perished at the hands of her mother, remembers auditioning for her part with Avy Kaufman. At that time, she was pre-screened as an option for Kyra, and was then brought back in for final auditions. Shyamalan at that time was already in pre-production in Philadelphia, and the small roles like Kyra were cast by Kaufman herself.

Barton, then thirteen, was virtually unknown, but once she appeared in *The Sixth Sense*, she would later play the memorable Marissa Cooper in *The O.C.*, which ran on Fox network for four seasons.

Barton recalls:

I was so young. I think I did actually go in [to meet Avy] and I don't think Night was there. I think it was just me and Avy. And then I went back after she pre screened me. She picked a couple of people, and then it kind of went up to Night and the final phase. I'm pretty sure he would have already been in pre-production between Philly and New York. There wasn't a ton of having to work things through with Night. He was great. He was just very busy. It was a huge undertaking, not just casting the small roles. It was a lot to do in terms of getting the set, like that [convention center, where they shot the majority of the interior shots] ready for all of his moving parts.

Olivia Williams rounded out the cast as Dr. Malcolm Crowe's wife. Williams started out at the Royal Shakespeare Company and the National Theatre, doing stage performances of the classics she had studied while attending Newnham College in Cambridge for English literature. She broke into television with a 1996 remake of *Emma* from the director Andrew Davies where she played Jane Fairfax, a character who made Emma envious of her physical attractiveness and accomplishments. The next year, Williams starred in *The Postman* with Kevin Costner. The movie is set in a post-apocalyptic America in 2013. Costner's character of the Postman, also known as Gordon Krantz, finds himself in possession of a postman's garb and mail bag and soon he takes on the identity of the mysterious postman, going to a nearby town to pose as someone he is not. He is soon seen by many in the nearby town as a glimmer of hope in a world on the brink of disaster, and he convinces neighbors to feed and care for him as he leads a community to a better existence. In *The Postman*, Williams plays Abby, a young woman who wants Krantz to impregnate her because her husband is infertile.

After *The Postman*, Williams appeared in Wes Anderson's film *Rushmore* opposite Jason Schwartzmann, Owen Wilson, Bill Murray, Connie Nielsen, and Luke Wilson. Williams played Rosemary Cross, a teacher who wins the affection of both Schwartzmann's character Max Fischer and Bill Murray's character Herman J. Blume, a father of one of Fischer's school friends. The film earned an 89 percent on

Rotten Tomatoes, and a lackluster $17 million at the box office on a $9 million budget.

And then, there was *The Sixth Sense*. After working with producer Barry Mendel on *Rushmore*, she was introduced to M. Night Shyamalan, who would work with Mendel on *The Sixth Sense*. Shyamalan thought she would fit perfectly for the role of Dr. Crowe's wife, bringing a certain class and understated demeanor that would make the audience sympathize with her husband's murder.

4

Filming in a Haunted Convention Center

When Shyamalan wrote the script for *The Sixth Sense*, he knew that he wanted to film in his hometown of Philadelphia, Pennsylvania. The city itself is full of history dating back to when it was founded in 1682 by William Penn, an English writer and religious thinker part of the Religious Society of Friends, also known as the Quakers. He came upon the land, previously inhabited by the Lenape Native Americans, after King Charles II gave what would become the states of Pennsylvania and Delaware to him in the form of a paid debt that the king owed to Penn's father, Sir William Penn, an admiral and politician.

Penn traveled up the Delaware Bay and the colonists there revered the man as their new proprietor, setting up the first Pennsylvania General Assembly. After this, Penn traveled further north to found Philadelphia. He signed a peace treaty with Lenape chief Tamanend, securing tolerance and human rights in writing. Two years later, however, a ship named *Isabella* arrived in the new city with hundreds of enslaved Africans. After four more years of slavery, local Quakers acknowledged the tension and signed the Germantown Petition Against Slavery, the first of its kind in the history of the New World.

Philadelphia became the biggest shipbuilding center of the colonies and, fast forward to the mid-1700s, attracted Benjamin Franklin and Thomas Paine, the latter releasing the leaflet "Common Sense." This would spark the Founding Fathers to declare independence in

1776 with the Declaration of Independence to be read for the first time in Philadelphia's State House, which is home to the Liberty Bell.

The city would serve as the capital of the United States after the Revolutionary War, harboring the most inhabitants of any other city in the colonies. The U.S. Constitution would be signed there in 1787 along with the establishment of the First Bank of the United States. Philadelphia's legacy for anti-slavery grew in the 1800s with William Lloyd Garrison creating the American Anti-Slavery Society.

And then came the Civil War, which pushed Philadelphia into the Union. Professionals in the city supplied weapons, uniforms, and warships during the perilous times. During the 1870s, Susan B. Anthony gave the Declaration of the Rights of Women outside Philadelphia's Independence Hall and the first U.S. zoo opened along with the Centennial Exhibition Fair, which honored 100 years since the signing of the Declaration of Independence. The Centennial Exhibition Fair, later known as the World's Fair, later took place in Chicago, New Orleans, and San Francisco, exalting each city's triumphs in arts and sciences.

Facing an economic boom during the Gilded Age, the population of Philadelphia soared until the Spanish Flu affected nearly 500,000 with over 60,000 dead over the period of a year. In the post–World War II era, population and jobs continued to decline and soon poverty and racial tensions followed in the early twentieth century, only to see it increase again decades later. After World War II, the city experienced a housing shortage where many buildings suffered from overcrowding and poor living conditions, and as time went on, the population decreased by 13 percent in the 1970s. Crime started to become a problem in the 1980s as mafia warfare increased as well as crack houses in parts of the city. When W. Wilson Goode, the first African American mayor, took over, new infrastructure around the city created skyscrapers that would shape the Old City. Unfortunately, the city would go into bankruptcy toward the end of the

1980s, but soon, Ed Rendell, the city's first Jewish mayor, would take over and turn the city around.

The decade of the 1990s was rocky for Rendell and Philadelphia residents, undertaking a budget deficit of $250 million. Luckily, Rendell enacted small budget surpluses and helped to stabilize Philadelphia's finances. Soon, a new convention opened, the city hosted the Republican National Convention, and tourism flourished, revitalizing the city after a long time of struggle. This would continue throughout the next few decades into the present day, where Philadelphia still relies on tourists to visit some historic places around the city.

Films such as *Rocky*, *Blow Out*, *Invincible*, and *Mannequin* were filmed in the city, and soon, filmmaker Shyamalan decided to film the majority of his movies there, too. Starting with *The Sixth Sense*, the writer/director chose to also set *Signs*, *The Happening*, *Lady in the Water*, *Unbreakable*, *Split*, and *Glass* in Philadelphia.

The interior shots of *The Sixth Sense* were filmed in the Philadelphia Convention Center, also known as the Municipal Auditorium. The massive structure was built in 1931 by Philip H. Johnson, an architect who also constructed other buildings in the city including the City Hall Annex as well as hospitals, libraries, firehouses, recreation centers, and National Guard armories.

The Municipal Auditorium was located at 3400 Civic Center Boulevard, close to the University of Pennsylvania and just southwest of Franklin Field. It held 12,000 people and was in art deco style. At the center, the city hosted the 1936 and 1948 Democratic National Conventions as well as the 1940 and 1948 Republican National Conventions. Martin Luther King Jr., Pope John Paul II, Nelson Mandela, and Lyndon B. Johnson spoke there and the Beatles and the Grateful Dead were among some of the popular bands that held concerts there. The center also held sports teams such as the Philadelphia Warriors, Philadelphia 76ers, Philadelphia Blazers, and minor-league Philadelphia Firebirds hockey team.

The auditorium seemed to be the best place for Shyamalan to film the majority of the interior scenes. From a disturbing scene where Mischa Barton famously vomits in Cole's red tent to the infamous scene where Cole tells Dr. Crowe "I see dead people," Shyamalan chose the historical sight to create the interior production design.

While filming, the younger actors like Barton, Osment, and Trevor Morgan took classes in the auditorium and spent off-hours playing in the hallways of what Barton claims is a "haunted" location.

"I don't know if it's just kids who make up that everything's haunted, but I'm pretty sure that place was haunted. Like, actually haunted," Barton said. "I don't really want to speak for Night, but I really think he kind of enjoyed it because it had this creepy air to it that made it even more fun."

Both Night and Osment agree that the center was spooky and reflected the paranormal aspects of the film.

"It was a very, very big building and most of it was empty, and so I can imagine for children that are running around there, it did feel very occupied spiritually," said Shyamalan. "A lot of corridors and empty, not great lighting, flickering bathrooms and things like that."

Osment said that it had a "kind of *The Shining* feel," with big, empty marble hallways and "cavernous, marble stairways that went really deep down."

Barton recalls seeing Osment throwing a ball against a wall as a game to pass the time between filming scenes. She remembered wanting to play with the boys and running around the large building on her own, rebelling against her teachers and adventuring the Municipal Auditorium.

The structure was later turned into the University of Pennsylvania Health System's Perelman Center for Advanced Medicine in 2008, a few years after *The Sixth Sense* was filmed there and the center was demolished in 2007.

Shyamalan filmed in a handful of other locations around the city to shoot the exterior scenes. One such location was at 2302 St. Alban's Place, which was built in the 1870s for industrial workers, known as the "Devil's Pocket." The neighborhood, which in the nineteenth century was known to be rough and full of Irish working-class Americans, was called the "Devil's Pocket" because a local priest at the time said that the children in the area were so gutsy that they would steal "the watch out of the Devil's pocket," they were so mischievous. At this house, Shyamalan filmed Dr. Crowe waiting outside, sitting on a bench, hoping to run into young Cole Sear. Willis is going through the child's file, learning about the boy before approaching him to tell him that he would be working with him to help cure his anxiety.

"We were actually on location scouting in our van and we were driving by here and I went 'Stop' and we jumped out and I was like 'This is amazing, this neighborhood. Look at this, it's amazing,'" Shyamalan told Josh Horowitz of Paramount Network for a YouTube video in 2019. "Maybe we could put a bench here and have him watching the kid. So, I jumped out. Probably the only location that I jumped out and was like, 'This is it.' Normally, I'm nauseous in the front seat and my head's down, but this time I was like, 'Look at that!'"

And then there's St. Augustine Church, where Dr. Crowe follows Cole to try to communicate with him and start their relationship as doctor/patient. Also known as "Old St. Augustine's," the Roman Catholic church was designed by Napoleon LeBrun and consecrated in the nineteenth century, displaying the Palladian-style architecture most famously seen in British buildings from the years 1715 to 1760. This type of design was created by sixteenth-century Italian architect Andrea Palladio, who was known to use symmetry, perspective, and principles seen in Ancient Roman and Greek design.

The building was the largest church in the city for some time, until Napoleon LeBrun designed another building, the Cathedral Basilica of Saints Peter and Paul, located in Philadelphia. The interior of the building features ceiling frescoes painted by Philip Costaggini, who painted the frieze on the rotunda of the Capitol in Washington, D.C. Shyamalan explains the reasoning behind choosing this church to Horowitz, saying that having a red door was imperative for the particular scene. St. Augustine's Chapel had just that.

"The idea of a red door was important. We used the color red a lot in the movie to signify awakening to another dimension, another world, another understanding of your existence," Shyamalan said.

Shyamalan went on to tell Horowitz that he chose to have Dr. Crowe and Cole speak for the first time in a church because of his time attending church and feeling safe as a child.

"I went to Catholic school for ten years, so it's really kind of embedded in me, these kinds of institutions. For the child to find safety in his mind, the character would go to where he perceives you're a little safer, which is in these churches," Shyamalan said.

Another key location for *The Sixth Sense* was Peirce College at 1420 Pine Street where Cole goes to elementary school. The building was built in 1915. The red brick establishment resonates with Shyamalan's vision of the color red symbolizing movement to another dimension. Now, the building caters to working adults who want to attend classes in their spare time. From healthcare management to accounting and criminal justice administration, Peirce College caters to a variety of studies to appeal to a wide range of scholars.

Isolated shots were filmed around Philadelphia, many of them focusing on male and female statues. A shot of Philly's Washington Monument on Benjamin Franklin Parkway makes an appearance before a breakfast scene between Cole and his mother, Lynn. The sculpture, designed by eighteenth-century artist Rudolf Siemering, pays tribute to George Washington who sits atop a fountain adorned with other replicas of men and women, some Native American, reflecting men and women who may have lived during his time.

Next is the Swann Memorial Fountain located in Logan Circle, which also depicts three Native American figures, two female and one male. Many Philadelphians swim in the fountain, designed and built in 1924 by Alexander Stirling Calder, the three statues symbolizing the three major waterways in the city. Shots of both the male and female statues appear after Cole sees three people hanging, dead, in his school and before a scene where Cole and his mother race through a grocery store parking lot, located at 601 W. Lancaster Avenue in Bryn Mawr.

Native Americans appear again in a shot of the ornamentation covering Philadelphia City Hall after a scene with Dr. Crowe and his wife having dinner at the now defunct Striped Bass restaurant at 1500 Walnut Street and a gruesome scene where Cole runs into a child ghost who has his head blown up by a gunshot wound. Shyamalan and the crew travel to Bryn Mawr as Cole and Dr. Crowe attend Kyra Collins' funeral, located 207 Rodney Circle, a quaint house in the suburbs of Philadelphia.

Each location, handpicked by Philadelphian Shyamalan, reflects motifs and thematic elements of the film. From red doors to historical statues around the city, Shyamalan grounds paranormal experiences and elements into the real world, linking the color red to incoming supernatural occurrences and showcasing Native American and American historical figures as "ghosts" of the past.

5

Cole Sear Interacts with the Dead

Even though *The Sixth Sense* scored a PG-13 rating, there is still some mature violent content present throughout the film. Ghosts are seen with bloody head wounds, cut wrists, and graphic burns, but the blood and gore is tame enough to keep the rating geared toward younger audiences, thirteen years of age and up. Shyamalan doesn't focus on the gore too much. *The Sixth Sense* isn't meant to be a slasher flick like *The Texas Chainsaw Massacre* or *A Nightmare on Elm Street*, both too graphic to retain a PG-13 MPAA rating. Shyamalan's film is instead focused more on the dramatic development of the characters, centering on thematic elements such as miscommunication between family members and love between the ensemble cast members. It is not gratuitously violent, and yet, it is still seen as a scary film with some scenes displaying violent imagery.

In the beginning of the film, Bruce Willis's Dr. Malcolm Crowe is shot by his ex-patient, Vincent Gray, played by malnourished, unhinged, and unrecognizable Donnie Wahlberg. Crowe falls to the bed, shot in the lower abdomen. The doctor holds his wound, and his wife, Olivia Williams's Anna Crowe, cries and screams, going to her husband to try to stop the bleeding. The camera pans back to Gray, who puts the gun to his head. Panning away from the ex-patient, we then hear a gunshot, subtly nodding to the fact that Gray has shot himself in the head, committing suicide. We do not see Gray actually do the deed and we do not see blood; we are just given context clues that the doctor is bleeding and Gray had killed himself. This is as far as Shyamalan wants to take the gore so far in the film.

Up until Haley Joel Osment's Cole Sear admits to Dr. Crowe that he sees dead people, we don't see any other gory scenes. There is a poltergeist occurrence in the Sear's kitchen in which Toni Collette's Lynn Sear walks into the kitchen to see all of the cabinetry had flown open on its own, but we aren't hit with anything bloody.

Just before Cole tells Malcolm his secret, there is a scene where Cole is at a character named Derrick's birthday party. This is the first time we see Cole actually interacting with a ghost. He sees a red balloon floating up to the top of a spiral staircase and decides to follow it. As he nears the top of the stairs, he hears a loud, angry voice coming from a crawlspace a few feet away from him. The voice is asking him to open the door to the crawl space. Cole is afraid. The camera then pans to Cole's bully Tommy Tammasimo along with another friend at the bottom of the stairs. The kids decide to go up and see what Cole is doing. Once they get to him, Tommy asks if Cole wants to be a part of a play in which he would be "locked in the dungeon." They proceed to grab Cole and stuff him in the crawlspace. Cole begins screaming until his mother hears him and goes upstairs to save him. She and her son are traumatized, and Lynn takes Cole to the hospital to get him checked out. At this point, we are not sure whose voice it was that Cole heard coming from the crawl space, but it's not long until we find out that the angry voice was a ghost.

In the next scene where Cole Sear is hospitalized and finally tells Dr. Crowe that he can see dead people, the young boy is sitting in his hospital bed with a blanket pulled up under his face. He looks exhausted and defeated while Dr. Crowe is trying to tell him a bedtime story. What starts as an innocent scene of Dr. Crowe trying to comfort Cole turns into a scene that would change the trajectory of the film from just a drama into something more paranormal and horrific. It would give birth to the iconic line "I see dead people" which would be quoted for decades after the success of the film.

According to Osment and makeup artist Michal Bigger, there was a scene attached to this clip with a ton of gore and violence that ended up being cut. In an interview with Rotten Tomatoes in 2019, Osment said that originally, the camera zoomed out after the hospital scene to a more "morbid" clip of other dead and dying patients with various severe injuries in the hospital.

Osment said:

> For this scene, I was just sitting in a bed doing the scene with Bruce and we're in an actual decommissioned hospital, but it was a very realistic and creepy place. There was an even more morbid element that ended up getting cut out. When I tell Bruce my secret, the last shot of the scene is pulled back from my bed and you look out the window where you can see another entire wing of the hospital and in every window there is a person with some horrible injury or someone who's gone and pale. So, you pull back and you see all these people sort of lined up on the other side of it and that was cut out of the movie, but everybody was on set that day with all this intense prosthetic makeup and horrible car accident victims and everything. The atmosphere was amazing, you had all these people walking around with these injuries when [Cole] tells [Malcolm] that these people are around all the time walking around like normal people and he's looking at dozens of them right past Bruce while he's telling him this, you don't see that in the movie, but for me, that was an added element.

Makeup artist Michal Bigger remembers this day of filming, but at the end of the day, he believes that Shyamalan made the right call by nixing the gratuitously gory scene, especially if the director wanted to attach a PG-13 label on the film to garner a more diverse audience.

"We did some massive scenes that never made it into the final cut, like the hospital full of dead and mangled people, but as much as I was attached to all the fabulous work the hair and makeup department put into it, I think the final cut down version was the most effective," Bigger said.

Right after this scene, Cole and Lynn come home from the hospital and Lynn puts her son to bed. She is holding her son's red sweater and realizes that it is ripped and torn. She lifts up her son's shirt to discover scratches all over his back. She is extremely concerned and calls one of the mothers from the birthday party to tell her to get her kids' "hands off" her son. In reality, we learn later that the ghosts were the ones giving Cole scratches and bruises all over his body.

The gore and violence in *The Sixth Sense* increase dramatically after Cole tells Malcolm that he can see dead people. We are in Cole's world now until the end of the film, with the exception of a few scenes where Malcolm is trying to get his wife's attention and make up for his seemingly crumbling marriage.

Cole wakes up in the middle of the night after returning to his home and has to use the bathroom. He timidly opens the door, looking out into the hallway before hobbling over to the bathroom where he relieves himself. The camera then pans to the thermostat, which is dramatically lowering in temperature. Any paranormal fanatic knows that when ghosts are around, the temperature drops. Shyamalan uses cold temperature to indicate that a ghost is around. The camera then goes back to Osment and while he urinates, we see a silhouette of a person walking behind Osment in the hallway and the background music suddenly erupts to give a jump scare. Osment turns and we can see his breath, it is that cold in the house. To achieve this visual breath, Shyamalan and the crew built a "cold room" where the staff would put a sheet over the set in the Philadelphia Convention

Center and pump freezing air into the room. They would use this method in a later scene with Mischa Barton, too.

Osment recalled:

> This was in the early days of CGI, and we didn't use CGI for the scenes where it was cold, and you could see our breath. What they did was they would drape this huge plastic sheeting over the sets and then pump in freezing cold air so that it would be below freezing, and you could see our breath. There was a limited time that we could be in there because it was so cold and most of the scenes I'm in my underwear or something. It's a tough environment, but it's great when you're in a scene where you're supposed to be frightened and shivering and it really is that cold. You can actually use real elements in those situations.

The cold room was so effective that Shyamalan said that even with CGI capabilities, he would probably still use the same methods he employed during the making of *The Sixth Sense*.

"CGI at that time was not perfected to the place where I felt comfortable that it could do breaths. So, we built a cold room. [Osment] wasn't acting, it was cold, and you could see the physicality on his skin and the way he's shivering. And even now, with CGI, I might do it the same way because of what it makes the actors do," Shyamalan said.

After we see the silhouette walk by the bathroom, Cole heads down the hallway to check things out. He enters the kitchen and thinks that he sees his mother, asking her if she had a bad dream about her husband, but when the camera pans to the figure, a woman with a bruised face, looking disgusted and angry, turns around. She is yelling at Cole as if he was her husband, saying, "Look what you made me do, Neddy!" The music intensifies and we see a close shot of the woman's wrists. Her arms have deep wounds, looking to be self-inflicted, as if the woman standing in the kitchen had killed her-self and is haunting Cole as the ghost of a battered woman. Cole quickly turns away from the screaming woman, running down the hallway to his sanctuary, a red tent set up in his room down the long hallway of the Sear home. The bloody wrists and battered face of this ghostly female apparition are enough to scare the crap out of anyone watching the movie. At this point, we are living in Cole's horrifying world, in disbelief that this child has to live every day seeing these kinds of gory figures wherever he goes.

The next day, Dr. Crowe is sitting in the back of Cole's school auditorium, watching a play in which Cole's bully, Tommy Tammasimo, is the lead. After the play finishes, the doctor and Cole are seen walking through the school hallway. Willis tells the boy that he thought the play was excellent, continuing to talk to Cole without realizing that something had stopped the boy from walking forward with him. The doctor turns around and walks back to find Cole, terrified standing in the hallway. The boy is visibly distraught, breathing heavily and looking down. He asks Malcolm if the doctor sees what he sees. The doctor says no, asking what he sees. Suddenly, the camera shifts down the hallway, showing three people hanging by nooses. According to an earlier scene, Cole told his teacher that lawmakers used to hang people in the building back before it was an elementary school. Now, we see these ghosts who met a gruesome demise. The music intensifies as the camera focuses on the three people hanging: a man, woman, and child. Shyamalan zooms in on their faces, all scratched up and bloody. Cole tells Malcolm to stay still, that it "gets cold" when the ghosts "get mad." He tells Malcolm that when your hairs stand up on the back of your neck, it means that ghosts are near. He asks the doctor to "please make them leave," to which Malcolm replies, "I'm working on it."

While Lynn Sear and Cole are having dinner, Lynn decides to confront her son about a "bumblebee pendant" which belonged to Cole's late grandmother, saying that she found the piece of jewelry in Cole's bedside table instead of its usual location with Lynn's things. She asks if the boy moved it there and he says, "No." At this point, Lynn still does not know that Cole can interact with dead people, but the viewer now knows his secret and can infer from this exchange that it was the ghost of his grandmother who moved the pendant, not the young boy. Cole has the opportunity to come clean about his secret, but chooses not to, even though it makes Lynn angry, believing that her son is lying. She yells at Cole to leave the table and he obliges.

Walking down the hallway to his room, he catches another glimpse of a silhouette. The figure comes out of the room and looks at Cole, saying, "I'll show you where my dad keeps his gun." The ghost boy turns around and we see a bloody head wound, pieces of brain and gore coming out of his head. This ghostly interaction sends Cole straight back to his mother, asking, "If you're not very mad, can I sleep in your bed tonight?" To which Lynn replies, "Look at my face, I'm not very mad." The two embrace and Lynn is extremely upset, asking Cole repeatedly to tell her what's wrong. He stays silent. He is not ready. At this point, the viewer is like Lynn, just wanting the kid to find some peace and open up to his loved ones.

While Malcolm is listening to tapes from his sessions with ex-patient-turned-murderer Vincent Gray, something that catches Malcolm's attention is when he says, "It's cold in here." Shortly after he says this, there is radio silence coming from the tape, but when Malcolm turns up the volume, he hears a third voice, neither Malcolm's nor Vincent's voice, saying "Yo no quiero morir," in English, "I don't want to die." He keeps rewinding the tape over and over again to try to confirm that this voice was actually there, and it was.

This kind of ghostly capture is called an Electronic Voice Phenomenon by ghosthunters and psychics. In the static of a voice note, we can sometimes hear audio from otherworldly sources. At this point, Malcolm realizes that Vincent may have also been able to see and speak with the dead, too. Gray and Sear are more alike than Malcolm could have ever imagined. The doctor is convinced that what the two boys experienced is real. Even though he wanted to drop Cole as a client, this realization turned his thinking around. He knows he has to help the boy just like he should have helped Vincent. This is his chance to change his karma. Instead of believing that this kid was just paranoid or schizophrenic, the doctor now realizes that it is much more complicated and unbelievable than that. Rather than drop Cole as a client, failing yet another patient, he is now driven to help Cole with his situation.

At the same church where Cole and Malcolm met for the first time, Malcolm finds the young boy again walking through the pews of the house of prayer. Cole rightly guesses that something happened to Malcolm that changed his thinking to believe the boy instead of dismiss him as hallucinating, to which Malcolm asks the boy, "Do you know what 'yo no quiero morir' means?" Cole does not know, but Malcolm does: it means, "I don't want to die." Malcolm then explains to Cole that the way to get the ghosts to go away is to help them. The doctor believes that each and every apparition comes to Cole with a need to help them solve something before they can pass on into the afterlife. Cole, at this point, believes that some of them just want to hurt others, but Malcolm rejects this hypothesis, saying, "I don't think that's how it works."

The next ghostly encounter of *The Sixth Sense* happens later that night, when Cole is sleeping with his dog in his red tent. He wakes up to the sound of his mother having a nightmare and goes to console her. She is having a dream about her son, asking, "Are they hurting you?" while tossing and turning in desperation. Cole puts his hand on her head, trying to calm her down by petting her hair. Just then, we can see Cole's breath again. Another "cold room" scene. Cole quickly goes to his tent to hide and is sobbing uncontrollably, so terrified. As he's sitting in his tent, something is ripping it apart at the seams, destroying his safe space. Suddenly, we see a young Mischa Barton as ghostly teenager Kyra Collins spewing vomit from her mouth. Cole is terrified, running away from the girl. Barton recalled shooting this scene and not being scared of the content. What is one of the scariest scenes in the film was no problem for the teenager to execute. Kyra's role was a dead girl who was poisoned daily by her mother, who had Munchausen by proxy syndrome. Barton was at that time familiar with the diagnosis, a terrifying real-life disorder that rips families apart.

"We would make a mixture to put in my mouth. They gave me options between cereals and bananas," Barton recalled of the substance she was spewing from her mouth to look like disgusting vomit. "And then, my mother [in the film] has Munchausen by proxy [syndrome] where you're poisoning your child, so that's a really intense thing, but creepy is part of my vernacular. It doesn't really bother me that much. I've always been fascinated by gothic and dark things. So, it wasn't like I was scared. It was more just really interesting subject matter. I've always felt like there's a real need to do the character justice. Everybody just asks, 'Was it traumatizing?' It really wasn't. I was already 13 and I could handle it."

We get to see Barton one more time in a following scene where Malcolm and Cole travel to Kyra's funeral reception in the suburbs outside of Philadelphia. The reception is well attended with dozens of actors playing funeral-goers, some talking about what a tragedy it is that the young girl was sick for so long and finally perished. Cole and Malcolm enter the house and go upstairs to the young girl's room. When Cole enters and starts looking around, a ghostly hand reaches out from under the bed, grabbing the young boy's ankles.

It's Kyra, and she has something for Cole: a box, containing a VHS tape. She is pale and sickly with bulging eyes and dark circles under them. She suffered greatly at the hands of her mother, a mentally ill caretaker who would lead her daughter to a premature death by prolonged exposure to poison placed in her lunches.

Cole gives the box to Kyra's father, who turns the video on in front of the rest of the funeral-goers. At first, it shows Kyra playing with her marionettes, and then, it shows Kyra running to her bed, pretending to be asleep while her mother pours poison into her soup on camera. Kyra must have figured out what was happening and decided to hide a camera to catch her mother in the act. Upon her death, she visited Cole because she needed help getting her father to confront her mother. Dr. Crowe was right about ghosts needing to be listened to. Mr. Collins watched the tape as well as the rest of the visitors there to mourn the death of this thirteen-year-old girl. He then approached his wife, who, of course, was wearing Shyamalan's signature color red on her clothes and lips to signify the thin line between reality and otherworldly occurrences, and Mr. Collins confronted her, saying, "You were keeping her sick." The mother looks in disbelief first at her husband and then at the rest of the attendees, all of them disgusted by her actions. Cole had done a good deed helping Kyra and Malcolm was right about the ghosts just wanting help, not coming from a place of malice.

Cole, invigorated by the good deed he did for Kyra Collins, appears in a school play, this time as a stable boy who is the only person in the village to be able to retrieve a sword stuck in a big rock in the middle of town, a take on the musical about a young King Arthur in *The Sword in the Stone*. Cole retrieves the sword and the rest of the village rejoices, lifting Cole up in their arms. The boy is the happiest he's been throughout the whole movie. Just before the play begins, we see Cole in the dressing room talking to a woman. Cole's teacher, the same one who Cole exasperatedly yelled at for being a "Stuttering Stanley," comes in as the woman gets up to leave. "Who are you talking to?" the teacher asks. The camera pans to the woman, who turns to show gruesome burns all over one side of her face and body. As she leaves, Cole lies, saying, "Just practicing my lines." The teacher and Cole leave the dressing room and head to the stage. The teacher tells Cole that there was a terrible fire in that section of the building that killed many people, to which Cole replies, "Yeah, I know." We then understand that the woman he was talking to must have been a victim in that fire.

The last gory encounter comes during the second to last scene where Cole and Lynn Sear are in standstill traffic in the middle of Philadelphia. Lynn is looking out the window to try to see what the holdup is. Cole already knows, and this time, he decides that it is finally time to tell his mother his "secrets."

"You know the accident up there? Someone got hurt. A lady. She died," Cole says.

"You can see her?" Lynn asks, puzzled.

"Standing next to my window."

The camera then shifts to Cole's side of the car where a woman is standing directly in front of him, bleeding from her head. She had been hit on the bike. This final piece of gore and blood lends itself to the resolution of the film, when Cole is ready to communicate with his mother and relieve the stress he had been carrying throughout his young life. Now, he's ready to share his burden with others, to own his gifts, and to finally communicate the truth with those who love him. Malcolm Crowe saved him. We now wonder, "What will life be like moving forward for Cole? Will ghosts still appear for him for the rest of his life?" We don't know the answer. The film is soon done. What we do know is that he won't have to carry his burden alone, and that is enough for the film to finally find resolution.

6

The Hardest Scenes to Film

The climax of *The Sixth Sense*, filmed in a car along 21st and Christian Street in Philadelphia, was what the cast and crew described as the most challenging four minutes to film throughout the entire movie.

In the famous "car scene," characters Lynn Sear (played by Toni Collette) and Cole Sear (played by Haley Joel Osment) are stuck in traffic in the middle of the Quaker City with Lynn becoming agitated that they are stuck and she can't see the cause of the holdup. As she is looking out her window, Cole decides that now is the time to share his secret with her.

"I'm ready to communicate with you," Cole says.

Lynn, confused, asks what he means. He responds that he wishes to "tell her his secrets."

At this point, the tension is high and there is no background music, which Shyamalan says a normal film would likely have during the climax.

"It's a four minute scene and there's no music. The traditional way to play the climax of the movie emotionally is to [have that] but there isn't a drop of music and these guys are just having this conversation in traffic," Shyamalan said in Charles Kiselyak's documentary, *"The Sixth Sense": Reflections From the Set*. "I remember thinking 'you could score this' but why? That was a big step as a filmmaker as well."

The viewer follows Lynn and Cole as they are communicating vaguely at first with Cole breadcrumbing his mother with hints to his secret. Soon, he says that he knows why there was traffic. A biker was just killed up ahead, and, suddenly, the camera pans to a ghost, a bloody woman who was just killed. She is wearing a helmet and exercise apparel, her face nearly split in half and pouring blood onto the sidewalk.

Osment plays this scene timidly, quietly, and with almost a sense of relief as he opens up to his mother. He is teary-eyed while Lynn is confused, unsure of how to deal with this newfound information about her son. Up until this point, she assumed that Cole was just dealing with anxiety and depression, unable to make friends because of his shy, anxious demeanor. Cole decides that rather than coming completely clean, saying "I see dead people," like he did when talking to Dr. Crowe about his secret, he wants to give proof to his mother that he can truly see the deceased, so he brings up his late grand-mother, telling Lynn that she "comes to him sometimes."

"Cole, that is very wrong," Collette says, concerned and in disbe-lief, adding that he is "scaring her." In this scene, Lynn is wearing a red sweater which matches her red hair. The color red, signifying the movement between dimensions and the existence of the paranor-mal, is again alluded to in this scene as Cole's mother wears the hue.

In Kiselyak's documentary, Collette says that the car scene was a defining reason why she decided to take the part of Lynn Sear. Throughout her journey playing Lynn, she felt herself developing maternal instincts that she had not previously explored, making the climax with Osment even more intense as she felt such a deep bond with the young actor, wanting to care for him as if he were her own son.

"Night was very adamant that [Lynn and Cole] were partners, not just mother and son. You don't talk down to him and he doesn't look up to you. You've got each other and that's it," Collette said in

Kiselyak's documentary. "I think it's strengthened from that scene in the car where he actually speaks honestly for the first time with her and lets her into his world."

Without music, the viewers instead follow the actors' raw emotions of the second to last scene. Collette and Osment, both breaking down in tears, felt that this scene took the biggest toll on them emotionally.

"That [scene] was one where we actually walked away from the day going, 'Gosh, I really hope we got that,'" Osment said. "We were feeling kind of nervous about it because it had been so hard."

Filming Osment's lines first, Shyamalan knew that this was one of the most important scenes in the whole film, so he pushed Osment to keep acting take after take until the late hours of filming to make sure that the ten-year-old performed exactly how Shyamalan envisioned for the dialogue between he and Collette.

"It was a very important scene for me. It may be that scene that takes you into another level of wherever you're going, writing that scene may have been the one taking you to a deeper place," Shyamalan said in Kiselyak's documentary. "The culmination of all the things I'd laid in about her Dad, about being a mom, the bumblebee pendant from the grandmother, it all comes together."

As Osment filmed his lines, Collette said that she could not control her emotions, feeling the intensity of the moment between mother and son. She weeps and holds her hands to her face as she cries, the enormity of this interaction hitting Collette hard as Cole explains to her what he sees every day, all the time. The maternal instincts of wanting to keep this child safe from harm made Collette seriously emotional as she put herself in her character's shoes with emotions of fear, grief, sadness, confusion, and overall overwhelm. Collette knew that this would be a tough scene to film, and at the end of the long day, everyone left nervous, wondering if they really got it.

"We did Haley's stuff first and I cried all the way through his takes," Collette said in Kiselyak's documentary. "It was just this unstoppable flow of something I had to let go of. I almost didn't have control over it."

"We did seven takes of it, and we just felt like we weren't getting it, and by the seventh one we felt like we had gotten some good stuff but there was still this unsureness," Osment told SYFY Wire in 2017.

Shyamalan recognized how much the scene was emotionally affecting both Collette and Osment, but he continued to push both of them until they got it right.

"I felt I had all the pieces, but I was not 100 percent sure, because we didn't do [the scene] in full takes that I felt comfortable with," Shyamalan said. At that point, he was filming Osment's lines over and over again and then Lynn's reactions over and over. There were not full takes of the scene, but as the day wore on, the actors and crew members were emotionally drained. It was time to stop and trust that they got what they needed. "We had to move on. I walked away, and I was talking to somebody else and then the AD came over and said 'Hey, they're both [Collette and Osment] really upset.' And I went back to the car and they were both crying and they said, 'Are you sure we got it? Are you sure we got it?' And I go, 'We got it,' and I gave them reassurance. I said, 'I'm pretty sure we got it.' And, we did get it," Shyamalan says.

The final cut of the four-minute-long scene shows Collette in full emotional breakdown, sobbing and putting her hands to her face in disbelief at what Osment tells her about her mother. To prove to Collette that he can see and speak to dead people, he says that Lynn's mother (his grandmother) watched her dance as a little girl and wanted to tell her, from the afterlife, that she is "proud" of her. Lynn, trying to process what her son is saying to her, just keeps crying. Through her tears, we get a sense that she is purging and working through a lot of deep-seated emotions and grief, from her divorce to her son's social anxiety to the death of her mother, and as she moves through this, we also see that Lynn is relieved perhaps just as much as Cole is. Likewise, we see that as Cole opens up to his mother about his "sixth sense," the truth finally coming out offers a breath of fresh air to the story that, as Shyamalan puts it, finally gives the film a "complete" resolution.

"[Haley's] not like a child, by the way, he is an analytical, intelligent, working, decision-making actor," Collette told the *Movie Show* in 1999. With the help of his father and direction from Shyamalan, along with his raw talent and intuitive performance capabilities, Osment shines as not just a child actor, but a professional actor with a bright future in the movie making business. Although this second to last scene lent itself to a peaceful resolution, Shyamalan was not done. He had one more trick up his sleeve.

Shyamalan says in Kiselyak's documentary:

> The structure of *The Sixth Sense*, to make it work perfectly, you have to have a resolution so complete and so fulfilling that you think the movie's over and that is the car scene for *The Sixth Sense*. For almost any movie, that is the end of the movie. [This] is a great, unbelievable ending to the movie when the child finally tells his secret to his mom. I had to think of that as the ending of the movie to make it carry the strength of everything so the next part felt like a Coda. People start to pack up their purses, drying their eyes, and then they go "What's going on here?"

The car scene, although it could have been the film's stopping point, lent itself to an even more intense ending, when the viewer sees Dr. Malcolm Crowe with his wife watching their wedding videos in their living room and the viewer learns that the doctor has been dead this whole time. This final scene would shock everyone who watched *The Sixth Sense*, either on home video or in the theaters, in the late nineties and into the new millennium. It would revolutionize thriller/horror movies and at the same time, put Shyamalan on the map as one of the most creative filmmakers of his generation. The twist, right after the car scene, would make *The Sixth Sense* memorable for generations to come.

For the cast and crew, the second to last scene became the most emotional day of filming that they had endured throughout the making of *The Sixth Sense*, and undoubtedly is what led Collette to receive an Academy Award nomination for her raw performance as Lynn Sear as she sits in the driver's seat of the car in full emotional breakdown; it became one of the most memorable performances of Collette's career. To this day, Collette is earning roles in major motion pictures as complicated mother figures, like Ari Aster's thriller *Hereditary*, Rian Johnson's Agatha Christie–esque murder mystery *Knives Out*, and the 2006 dramedy *Little Miss Sunshine* with Abigail Breslin and Steve Carell. Her characters are as unlikable as they are captivating, with Collette delivering memorable performances which would be recognized over and over again at major awards shows.

The car scene wasn't the only difficult day of filming, however. In Kiselyak's documentary, Haley Joel Osment recalled another tough scene where Dr. Malcolm Crowe tells Cole Sear that he can no longer be his therapist. Cole and Dr. Crowe stand opposite each other in Cole's school hallway and the young boy asks his doctor what he wants more than anything in this world. The doctor, still unaware that he is dead, tells the boy that he wants to communicate and spend more time with his wife. He tells Cole that he can only do this if he lets go of working so hard and puts his marriage first.

"I haven't given my family enough attention. Bad things happen when you do that. Do you understand?" Dr. Crowe asks the boy.

Cole becomes fearful and the waterworks start. At this point, Cole feels like Dr. Crowe is the only person in his life that can understand his plight and help him deal with his "sixth sense." He doesn't trust anyone else with his secret. In this scene, he worries that he will be abandoned by Dr. Crowe, just like he was abandoned by his father.

"Don't fail me. Don't give up, you're the only one who can help me. I know it," the boy says. Vincent Gray said something similar in the beginning scene of *The Sixth Sense*, showing the parallels between characters. Dr. Crowe, with Cole Sear, has another chance to make things right.

This clip was one of the hardest scenes to film for both Osment and Willis, but especially for the child star. He had to access strong emotions on cue, adhering to Shyamalan's direction all the way through. Early on in filming, Shyamalan told Osment that his character should never show sadness, but instead rely on fear and anger as primary emotions. This may have not been intuitive in this scene as one would expect Cole to be sad about his doctor's sudden abandonment. Cole had to play it with emotions of fear and anger instead. He is terrified that he will see dead people for the rest of his life, unable to open up to those closest to him. Being fearful instead of sad during this scene was a challenge for Osment. Although Cole may have been sad to lose his doctor, he is more terrified that he might have to live with his supernatural abilities for the rest of his life, hiding it from the rest of the world for fear of being deemed a "freak" by his peers and family. Osment worked on projecting this fear on camera and behind the scenes, working tirelessly on his lines with his father, who was with Haley Joel throughout production.

"Cole's emotions reach the highest point where he gets the most scared because this doctor's come into his life and has given him the first glimpse that maybe there's a way out of being scared all the time. And then, it's going away," Osment recalls in Kiselyak's documentary. "That type of fear, a fear even beyond what he's been experiencing all his life, was challenging. I spent a lot of time in rehearsal, the night before with my dad studying all the scenes preceding it and the scenes after it to see what kind of tones had to be there in the scene and seeing what special things that would affect things coming after it."

"The first take, I wasn't happy with. I really had to pound it out. It was really the highest point I'd ever gone with really emotionally pumping myself up for the scene. It turned out to be one of the scenes of greatest heartbreak because that was sort of where the light at the end of the tunnel was being closed off from him."

On Willis's end, he wanted to give Shyamalan several scenes to work with. Take by take, he transformed. Willis said that there were shots of him bawling his eyes out, in tears, and shots of him composed, unaffected and rationally minded when dealing with abandoning yet another client.

"It was a really emotional day. Some of the crew was crying. We kept going to the point where I wasn't crying at all. We did a couple takes like that," Willis said in Kiselyak's documentary. "I wanted Night to have as many options as he could. I'm not that big of a fan of what I call 'wet scenes' where everybody's just crying all over the joint. Those scenes do exist of me bawling my eyes out, but thank God they're not in the movie because I just think it wasn't right for the character."

At the end of the day, Osment cries in fear while Willis tells him he must leave him in a week's time, and Shyamalan picks a take where Willis is teary-eyed at best, showing that the doctor is empathetic, but stoic and firm in his decision.

7

The Art of the Twist

Before Shyamalan shocked viewers with his twist ending in *The Sixth Sense*, other films like *Star Wars Episode V: The Empire Strikes Back*, released in 1980, and *Scream* in 1996 were using twist endings to try to get moviegoers back into the theaters for multiple viewings, but like Spielberg told Joe Roth and Night one evening, Shyamalan was truly the first one to accomplish this. Having said that, these other films were successful in their own right, spooking the crowds and creating memorable endings to be respected and heralded as truly revolutionary for decades to come.

In *Star Wars Episode V: The Empire Strikes Back*, we see villain Darth Vader and his empire of storm troopers and admirals trying to thwart the actions of the Freedom Fighters of the galaxy, including Princess Leia played by Carrie Fisher, Luke Skywalker played by Mark Hamill, Han Solo played by Harrison Ford, Chewbacca played by Peter Mayhew, C-3PO played by Anthony Daniels, and R2-D2 played by Kenny Baker. We see Vader on a mission to find Luke Skywalker and defeat the rest of the clan, but the kid is always just out of his reach. In *The Empire Strikes Back* we see Luke getting telepathic messages from the late Obi Wan Kenobi, known to Luke as "Ben," who tells the young aspiring Jedi master (an accomplished fighter who uses the powers of the Force for good) to go to the Dagobah system (a swampy planet across the galaxy) to find a Jedi master named Yoda, played by Deep Roy and Frank Oz in the film, and get trained by him to become a Jedi master capable of defeating Darth Vader and putting an end to the evil forces out to destroy good.

In this film, we are hit with one of the first cinematic twists that really floored viewers. No one saw it coming, and it, like *The Sixth Sense* sparked a particular line in the film becoming memorable and meme worthy for decades to come. At the end of *Star Wars Episode V: The Empire Strikes Back*, Luke Skywalker and Darth Vader are fighting with their light sabers. The film is action-packed all the way through, but the finale, featuring the young Luke and the evil Vader, keeps you on the edge of your seat. After Vader severs Luke's hand in a fight and as he hangs from a structure in Darth Vader's ship, known as the *Executor*, the villain says to him, "I am your father," following it up with "Your destiny lies with me, Skywalker." The revelation that Luke's father is Darth Vader, the most evil man in the galaxy, sends Luke into a tailspin, and as the villain asks his son to join him, Luke refuses and lets go of the structure and into a free fall through the bowels of the ship.

"I am your father"—the simple line that would be quoted endlessly since the film's premiere in 1980—set cinema up for all of the twist endings that would follow through the years. Darth Vader became an icon in filmography with the deep, commanding voice and signature black helmet, inspiring Halloween costumes for years, even decades, to come. The line, like Shyamalan's "I see dead people," would lead to a cultural phenomenon, heralded by *Washington Post* staff writer Gary Arnold in 1980 as "a pop culture phenomenon that shouldn't be missed.

"*Empire* is a thrilling, witty, inventive continuation of *Star Wars* but it also introduces a more serious approach and springs an astonishing plot twist, which promises to keep audiences buzzing and open up the story for deeper dramatic exploitation," Arnold continues. "Surprises are in store, perhaps unwelcome if you hoped for a strictly ingratiating reprise of the original movie—but potentially electrifying if you care for a new departure."

Indeed, the original *Star Wars* did not end on the same level of plot twist that this one did. *Empire* was revolutionary in its own right, leaving viewers yearning for the follow-up in 1983, *Star Wars Episode VI: The Return of the Jedi*.

"A more impressive and harrowing magic carpet ride than its fundamentally endearing predecessor, *Empire* pulls the carpet out from under you while simultaneously soaring alone," writes Arnold.

In 1996, we saw another successful take on the plot twist in the form of legendary horror director Wes Craven's slasher flick *Scream* starring Neve Campbell, Courteney Cox, David Arquette, Rose McGowan, Matthew Lillard, Skeet Ulrich, and a brief appearance from Drew Barrymore, who becomes the first one killed in the film.

Craven is known for his successful horror movies, churning out the cult classic *A Nightmare on Elm Street*, *The Last House on the Left*, and *The Hills Have Eyes*, all of which use blood and gore to an extreme, making him one of the most prolific slasher directors in history. *Scream* pokes fun at scary movie plots, each of the characters talking openly about how they are in a horror movie, cracking jokes about Hollywood stereotypes. The blond virgin always gets murdered, and in *Scream*, that is true. The film opens with Barrymore's blond, high-school aged character Casey Becker alone at her house, making popcorn on the stove top. She gets a call from an unknown number and on the other end is a scary-sounding man asking her if she "likes scary movies." She plays along with this stranger, who then asks her if she has a boyfriend and what her name is. "Why?" she asks. "I want to know who I'm looking at," he replies. Tense music ensues as Casey looks around, trying to find the potential intruder. "You hang up on me again and I'll gut you like a fish," the strange voice says menacingly, causing Casey to freak out and run around the house making sure that every door is locked. "What do you want?" Casey asks. "To see what your insides look like," replies the soon-to-be killer.

Casey is stunned and screaming, saying that her boyfriend will be there soon. The intruder asks if her boyfriend is named Steve. Casey is stunned, turning the patio lights on to see her boyfriend, Steve, tied to a chair and gagged with duct tape around his mouth. The intruder wants to play a game, asking Casey trivia about horror movies. He asks her a warm-up question. Who is the main character in the movie *Halloween*? "Michael Myers!" Casey screams. She's right. The strange man asks her who the killer is in *Friday the 13th*. She guesses Jason Voorhees and she is wrong, it's actually Jason's mother, Mrs. Voorhees. Because she guesses wrong, Steve is immediately slashed by the killer, his insides pouring out of him in true Wes Craven fashion. Total gore. Suddenly, Casey sees him, a man dressed in a black costume with a white mask over his face. At this point, we meet Ghostface, the slasher killer of Craven's *Scream*. He throws a chair into Casey's window and the girl screams, grabbing a knife and running outside. Ghostface chases her and eventually stabs her in the chest. At that moment, Casey's parents return home, but Casey is breathless, screaming with no sound coming out of her mouth. Ghostface jumps on Casey again, stabbing her repeatedly while her parents are inside, frantically trying to find her. Casey's mother leaves the house and sees Casey hanging from a tree with her insides outside of her body, just like Steve. The first scene of *Scream* sets the slasher up to be a wild roller coaster ride led by Craven and the rest of the ensemble cast, with Neve Campbell shining as Sidney Prescott, a high school student whose mother was murdered a year before Ghostface started stalking the small town of Woodsboro.

As noted by renowned film critic Roger Ebert, *Scream* is a movie about a horror movie, a unique take on moviemaking. After Casey and Steve die in the first scene, journalists like Courteney Cox's character Gale Weathers are on the scene at the school, trying to

In the beginning scene of The Sixth Sense, *Dr. Malcolm Crowe and his wife, Anna, are seen in their bedroom, but they are not alone. A disheveled and emaciated Vincent Gray, one of Dr. Crowe's ex-patients, has snuck into their home and is there to kill the doctor.* BUENA VISTA / PHOTOFEST © BUENA VISTA

Donnie Wahlberg lost a considerable amount of weight for the role of Vincent Gray, Dr. Malcolm Crowe's old patient. At the beginning of the film, we see Gray shoot Dr. Crowe in cold blood because he believed the psychologist "failed" him. BUENA VISTA / PHOTOFEST © BUENA VISTA

Bruce Willis and Haley Joel Osment stroll through the streets of Philadelphia. PICTURELUX / ALAMY STOCK PHOTO

Haley Joel Osment's character Cole Sear spends some time praying in a Philadelphia chapel, wearing wide frame glasses belonging to his estranged father. ENTERTAINMENT PICTURES / ALAMY STOCK PHOTO

Toni Collette's character, Lynn Sear, and Osment's Cole Sear enjoy a breakfast together before Cole heads to school. MAXIMUM FILM / ALAMY STOCK PHOTO

Haley Joel Osment can see his own breath as he encounters ghosts in his home who are manipulating the temperature. In order to achieve this effect, Shyamalan built "cold rooms" on set at the Philadelphia Convention Center, blasting the actors with cold air instead of using CGI. ZUMA PRESS, INC. / ALAMY STOCK PHOTO

Haley Joel Osment lays in a hospital bed, talking to Bruce Willis's Dr. Malcolm Crowe. In this scene, he utters the famous line "I see dead people." MOVIESTORE COLLECTION / ALAMY STOCK PHOTO

Osment and Willis are seen at Cole Sear's school, where the young boy tells the doctor that he can see ghosts at the end of the hallway. BUENA VISTA / PHOTOFEST © BUENA VISTA

*Bruce Willis
and Haley Joel
Osment arrive
at a funeral
reception for
Mischa Barton's
character Kyra
Collins, heading
upstairs to
the dead girl's
bedroom looking
for clues to help
her spirit pass
on.* IFA FILM /
ALAMY STOCK
PHOTO

*Mischa Barton,
who plays
dead girl Kyra
Collins, is found
underneath her
bed as Osment
and Willis try to
connect with her
at her funeral
reception.*
BUENA VISTA /
PHOTOFEST ©
BUENA VISTA

*Both Osment
and Collette
agree that the
"car scene" at
the end of the
movie was the
hardest to film.
Both in tears,
the actors tried
to perfect the
scene, working
take after
take to get it
right.* BUENA
VISTA / PHOTOFEST
© BUENA VISTA

Willis and Shyamalan developed a friendship that would last decades. The Sixth Sense was the duo's first movie together. Willis would later work on Unbreakable, Glass, *and* Split *with the legendary director.* BUENA VISTA / PHOTOFEST © BUENA VISTA

Collette said that her relationship with Osment was not only maternal, but also professional. She treated the young boy like the serious actor he was. BUENA VISTA / PHOTOFEST © BUENA VISTA

Bruce Willis, M. Night Shyamalan, and Haley Joel Osment pose for the camera after winning awards for the making of The Sixth Sense. ROSE PROUSER / ALAMY STOCK PHOTO

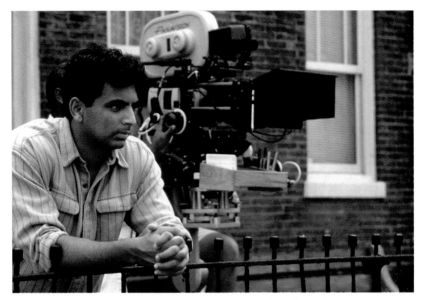

According to many who have worked with Shyamalan, the Indian American filmmaker knows what he wants and is determined to get it. He is careful about the choices he makes as a moviemaker, and still has the energy and audacity to make the sets fun-loving and collaborative. MAXIMUM FILM / ALAMY STOCK PHOTO

The Sixth Sense *propelled Shyamalan into superstardom as a profound, revolutionary director. The filmmaker would go on to have a memorable career, with both flops and hits under his belt.* BUENA VISTA / PHOTOFEST © BUENA VISTA

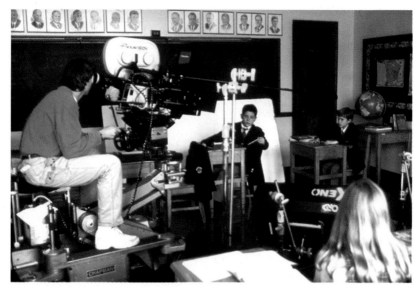

The crew members of The Sixth Sense *set up a scene at Cole Sear's school. Most interior scenes were shot at the Philadelphia Convention Center, with many sources claiming the building was haunted. It was torn down shortly after the making of the film.* BUENA VISTA / PHOTOFEST © BUENA VISTA

Shyamalan is a hands-on director who knows what he wants, but is also open to suggestions from the cast. Willis and Shyamalan worked together on the role of Dr. Malcolm Crowe. BUENA VISTA / PHOTOFEST © BUENA VISTA

interview students about the stabbings to get their fifteen minutes of fame covering the small-town murders. The kids at the school start joking about who will get murdered next based on scary movie clichés. One particular student, Randy Meeks, played by Jamie Kennedy, actually works at a video store and frequently jokes about how the brutal happenings mirror classic horror films. At one point, the student says that blonde virgins always get murdered first, just like Casey Becker, and how, if you don't want to be murdered, you must refrain from having sex, doing drugs, drinking booze, and going anywhere alone. Tatum, played by McGowan, even jokes around with Neve Campbell's character, asking who she would be played by in a movie rendition of the town's massacre. The deputy Dewey Riley (played by David Arquette) says, "I see you as a young Meg Ryan, myself," to which Campbell replies, "Thanks, Dewey, but with my luck I'd get Tori Spelling."

"*Scream* is about knowledge of the movies: The characters in *Scream* are in a horror film, and because they've seen so many horror films, they know what to do, and what not to do," Ebert writes. "Don't say 'I'll be right back,' one kid advises a friend, 'because whenever anybody says that, he's never right back.' In a way, this movie was inevitable. A lot of modern film criticism involves 'deconstruction' of movie plots. 'Deconstruction' is an academic word. It means saying what everybody knows about the movies in words nobody can understand. *Scream* is self-deconstructing; it's like one of those cans that heats its own soup."

In fact, the movie reveals the true killer early on in the film. Prescott's boyfriend, Billy Loomis, played by Skeet Ulrich, is seen coming through Prescott's window just after she gets attacked by Ghostface. He's at the scene, and as he tries to console her, a cellular phone drops out of his pocket. Ghostface had just called her right before Loomis showed up. Prescott is terrified and calls the police, who arrest Loomis early in the film. The camera cuts to Loomis in the interrogation room with a police officer and his father. He claims emphatically that he did not make the calls to Sidney, and upon checking the phone records, it seems he really didn't make the calls, so he is released. At this point, the viewer thinks that, although he is very suspicious, he didn't make the calls to Sidney's phone as Ghostface, so we write him off as innocent. Big mistake.

Ghostface goes on to kill the school's principal, played by Henry Winkler, stabbing him to death in his office. The kids don't find this out until they are all at a party that night and Randy gets a call that the principal is dead. The party scenes bring together the entirety of the ensemble cast, with McGowan acting a particularly memorable scene with Ghostface in the garage. "Don't kill me, Mr. Ghostface, I wanna be in the sequel!" She jokes around with the killer, who she thinks at that point can't be real but another kid mocking the murderer. He is, in fact, the masked killer, and he proceeds to chase her around the garage while she fights back, throwing beer bottles at him. When she tries to escape through the doggy door, Ghostface turns on the garage doors to make them lift. Tatum is now suspended in the air and is crushed when the door lifts all the way up and splits her in half.

Meanwhile, Sidney and her boyfriend Billy are upstairs in a bedroom and Sidney apologizes for her PTSD that resulted from her mother's rape and murder affecting their relationship. Billy then apologizes as well for his selfishness. The teenagers decide that they want to sleep together for the first time and while they are having sex, the camera cuts to Deputy Dewey and Gale Weathers finding Sidney's father's abandoned vehicle close to the party house. Up until this point, Sidney's father has been labeled the prime suspect of the murders. He left to go to a work conference at the beginning of the film and hasn't been heard from since. Finding his abandoned car is a huge clue that the man must not be far away. If he is indeed the killer, he's definitely on the premises.

Cut back to Sidney and Billy in bed, putting on their clothes again. They are talking about the killer and Sidney speaks as if she still suspects the teenager of the murders. He says, "What do I have to do to prove to you that I'm not a killer?" After this moment, Ghostface enters the room and stabs Billy. Sidney screams, running to escape through the window. She jumps down and when she gets up, she sees Tatum's dead body hanging from the garage doors. She continues running, jumping over a fence and into the street. Gale Weathers, in the meantime, runs to her van and hops in, seeing blood everywhere. When she starts the van and guns it, her cameraman's body is bloody and mutilated, falling into the windshield. Gale continues to drive, screaming, and Sidney sees the van, jumping into the street. Gale narrowly misses her and the van veers off the road. Sidney continues running and ends up back in the front yard of the house, where she sees both Randy and Stu Macher, played by Matthew Lillard. At this point, Sidney trusts no one. She has a gun in her hand and Randy says that Stu is the killer and tells her to shoot him. She doesn't, and instead runs back into the house.

Billy, to everyone's surprise, is still alive and fumbling down the stairs to meet Sidney. When he gets downstairs, Randy and Stu both find a way in and Sidney is faced with Billy, Randy, and Stu. Billy has a gun, too, and shoots Randy point blank in the entryway. "We all go a little mad sometimes," Billy says, licking his bloody fingers. "Mmm, corn syrup. Same stuff they used for pig's blood in *Carrie*." Stu says, "Surprise, Sidney." At this point, Sidney along with the viewer figure out that both Stu and Billy are the killers. Why did they do it? Sidney's mother was having an affair with Billy's dad, which led to Billy's mother leaving him. He says that maternal abandonment makes people psychotic. Both he and Stu raped and killed Sidney's mother a year prior, and on the anniversary of her killing, they wanted to go on a killing spree, leaving a wake of blood and gore in their path. They framed a man named Cotton Weary, who was also having an affair with Sidney's mom, and he, in turn, is at the time waiting for trial. Stu heads into a closet and retrieves Sidney's father, whose hands and feet are tied and mouth covered with duct tape. Her father was not the killer, but Billy and Stu intend to frame him for all the murders. Billy starts to stab Stu, but does it too deeply, leaving Stu in pain and dying. Billy then goes for Sidney, almost slashing her to bits, but luckily, Gale Weathers comes through the door with a gun and shoots Billy. Gale, Randy, Sidney, Sidney's father, and Deputy Dewey all survive the attack, leaving Billy and Stu to die in the house. *Scream*'s twist and memorable lines like "Do you like scary movies?" made this nineties flick a film to remember, also inspiring many sequels with twists and turns just as successfully executed as the original film. Three more films, *Scream 2*, *Scream 3*, and *Scream 4*, were released in 1997, 2000, and 2011, respectively. The cast and crew got back together a decade later in 2022 for a remake of the original, and another film, *Scream 6* is set to be released in 2023.

Another film released in 1996 with a killer twist ending was *Primal Fear*, starring Richard Gere, Edward Norton, John Mahoney, Frances McDormand, and Laura Linney. The movie was produced by Paramount Pictures, raking in $56 million on a $30 million budget, scoring a 77 percent on Rotten Tomatoes. The screenplay was based on a novel by William Diehl with the same name. The story follows Gere's character Martin Vail, a hotshot Chicago-based attorney, who decides to take a case involving Edward Norton's character Aaron Stampler pro bono. Vail sees Stampler on the news running away from a murder scene with blood all over him. For whatever reason, he is drawn to Stampler and wants to represent his case. Stampler, an altar boy, is accused of murdering Archbishop Rushman of Chicago.

When Vail goes to meet Stampler in jail, the altar boy seems innocent, quiet, and shy, with a severe stutter. "He was like a father to me," says Stampler of the archbishop. He claims that there was someone else in the room with him when the archbishop was murdered. Stampler was just there to return a book. He tells Vail that he "blacked out" and "lost time," something typical of Stampler. He ran from the scene because he was "scared."

Soon, Stampler is referred to in the news as "The Butcher Boy of St. Mike's," immediately presumed guilty even before the altar boy went to trial. Vail's team is sure that the boy is faking the story, that it's all bullshit, but Vail is determined to represent him regardless. Vail knows that the prosecution doesn't have motive and must prove reasonable doubt, which Vail doesn't believe they'll be able to prove. Vail knows that he must bring on a psychiatrist who knows about amnesia to prove that Stampler indeed suffers from black outs where he can't remember what he did. In comes Frances McDormand, who plays the psychiatrist Molly in *Primal Fear*. "He looks like a boy scout," Molly says. For a major chunk of the movie, we see Stampler interacting with Molly, talking about how his blackouts started when he was twelve, along with his stuttering. He tells Molly that his mother died and his father was "not a nice man." To the psychiatrist, Stampler seems like a troubled, shy boy who sought refuge in the church with the archbishop taking the place of his violent father. He doesn't seem like a killer.

During the trial, we find out that State Attorney John Shaughnessy, played by Mahoney, had motive to kill the archbishop. The two were in cahoots on financial dealings that went bad, leading to millions of dollars down the drain. This plot twist serves as a red herring, forcing us to consider Shaughnessy as the primary suspect. The prosecution, in response, highlights a piece of evidence that the defense team overlooked. "B32 156," which was carved into the archbishop's chest, refers to a book from his library, *The Scarlet Letter* by Nathaniel Hawthorne. Upon investigation, the prosecution found an underlined passage in the book about a certain person being two-faced and dishonest. The suspect must have seen the archbishop as two-faced, but why? When asked about the passage, Stampler denies that he underlined it, saying that he doesn't like Hawthorne.

And then, the film takes a few unexpected turns that the audience didn't see coming. While meeting with Molly, a new, evil side of Stampler makes an appearance. She wants to keep talking to him, but he says he's tired and his head hurts. She goes to the camera, saying, "You know what I can do with this?" To which Stampler raises his eyes and looks menacingly at her, saying, "How the fuck should I know?" This is a totally new side of Stampler that did not match his quiet, shy demeanor as Aaron. No, this is someone else entirely, a new personality unlocked. This is Roy, Aaron's alter ego. While in this state, he tells both Vail and Molly that the archbishop forced him to tape sexual encounters, which he called "purging the devil." He was traumatized, clearly, from this event, and at the end of the day, it gave the defense motive. While in this alter ego, he tells Vail that "Aaron's crying off in a corner somewhere" and that "Aaron don't have the guts to do nothing. It was me, boy." In this scene, Roy confesses to murdering Archbishop Rushman. Unfortunately, for Vail's team, it's too late into the trial to switch to an insanity defense, which is already nearly impossible to prove, anyway. Vail decides, at this point, to send the tape straight to Laura Linney's character, Janet Venable, the lead prosecutor on the case. In this way, yes, the prosecution has their motive, but the tape also makes Stampler look like a "sad, abused boy."

On trial, Vail calls Molly to the stand, who testifies that Stampler suffers from multiple personalities. She has no direct proof of this, though, as the camera was not turned on when Roy made his appearance to her and Vail in the interrogation room. She does say that Aaron knows right from wrong, but it was Roy who murdered Archbishop Rushman, not Aaron. At this point, Venable and Judge Shoat, played by Alfre Woodard, are against this testimony, both saying that it is too late in the trial to switch to a plea of insanity. As a last witness, Vail decides to call Stampler to the stand. It is rare for a defendant to take the stand, but in this case, Vail has a plan. He's going to try to bring Roy out of Aaron to show the jury that he indeed is insane and would be better suited in an institution than a jail cell.

As Vail is questioning Aaron, he goes up to the stand, covering the microphone with his hand, and says to Aaron, "Stop whining, be a man." Aaron is shocked as Vail eggs him on. Vail asks if he knows Roy, to which Aaron says no. Vail finishes his questioning and it's time for Venable to cross-examine him. In front of the jury, Venable asks Stampler about *The Scarlet Letter* underlined passage. "Do you believe that the archbishop wore masks?" Stampler replies, "No, I did not think that. I did not underline that book." She then brings up the sex tape, saying to Stampler that Archbishop Rushman needed him "to perform like a circus animal." This frustrates Aaron and Venable keeps egging him on, saying that Rushman "forced" him to perform the sex acts and videotape them. She gets angrier and angrier, saying, "He forced you using a threat of expulsion from Savior House and a life on the street with no heat, no water and no food. He put you in front of a camera! He made you take off your clothes!" She says that this behavior would have made her angry too, angry enough to kill. "I would stab him 78 times with a butcher knife! I would chop off his fingers! I would slash his throat open! I would carve numbers into his chest! I would gouge out his eyes! But that's me."

Venable's tirade was enough to push Aaron over the edge and do exactly what Vail intended on him to do: bring Roy out to show the jury that he was insane.

"Where the hell are you going?" Roy yells to Venable as she's going back to her bench. "Look at me when I'm talking to you, bitch!"

Roy leaps from the witness stand and attacks Venable, grabbing her by the neck. The courtroom erupts as Roy shows himself to the crowd. His alter ego has emerged, just as Vail thought. As the bailiffs pry Roy from Venable, the courtroom now has a different vision of who Aaron Stampler really is: a psychotic lunatic with multiple personality disorder.

After this circus, Judge Shoat tells Vail that she's going to dismiss the jury in favor of a bench trial and a plea of not guilty by reason of insanity. Vail won. He goes to see Stampler after the trial to tell the defendant the good news. Stampler is elated and grateful, but the movie's not done there. As Vail leaves the cell, Stampler says, "Will you tell Miss Venable I'm sorry? Tell her I hope her neck is okay."

"What did you just say? You told me you don't remember. You black out. So, how do you know about her neck?" Vail responds.

Stampler starts clapping slowly. "Well, good for you, Marty. I was going to let it go. You were looking so happy just now. To tell you the truth, I'm glad you figured it out. Because I've been dying to tell you. I just didn't know who you'd want to hear it from, Aaron or Roy, Roy or Aaron."

He then goes on to confess to murder of the archbishop as well as the murder of his "girlfriend" Linda, who was in the sex tapes with him.

"So , there never was a Roy?" Vail asks.

"Jesus Christ, Marty. If that's what you think, I'm disappointed in you. There never was an Aaron, counselor."

Vail is flabbergasted along with the viewer, who sympathized with Aaron throughout the course of the movie. Up until this point, we were sure that the meek kid, Aaron Stampler, was the primary personality of this insane man. Instead, we learn that Roy is the main personality, the psychotic, evil, abusive man. The twist is a memorable one, another that we did not see coming. We are as shocked as Gere's character. Now, this evil man is loose yet again, sure to commit more murders now that he is free.

In a conversation on CinemaBlend's podcast ReelBlend in 2020, Norton recalls being a virtually unknown actor when he appeared in

Primal Fear in 1996. He said that because he was unfamiliar to the audience, viewers didn't know which was his real voice and which was an act, which made the twist all the more powerful.

Norton said:

> "*Primal Fear* is about someone who's a really good actor who's burning somebody else. What was fun about it was knowing that it's only gonna happen once, no one knows who you are. Nobody knows anything about you. They don't know what your real voice is, so you can get away with murder, literally. We were having a lot of fun with that. If I was proud of something, when we were trying to think of, Well, what's going to annihilate suspicion or what makes you think immediately like "Oh my God, this poor person, the fact that he can barely get his words out, he's stuttering so horribly," is so manipulative since it's not actually true. It's like this incredibly great manipulation on slick Richard Gere. What I liked about it was I knew no one would know what to make of it. It's like, they haven't seen you in anything. I always think, when an audience can have the same experience as the lead character, it's kind of great. They're like Richard Gere, they're like, "This poor guy. This poor kid. He deserves our help," you know what I mean? He's sick, he's really messed up and so on and so forth. So, the shock Richard Gere experiences at the end of the film, the audience is experiencing.

Twist endings featuring men with multiple personality disorders were made popular by not only *Primal Fear*, but also with *Fight Club* in 1999 and *Shutter Island* in 2010. *Fight Club*, again starring Edward Norton alongside Brad Pitt, Helena Bonham Carter, Jared Leto, and Meat Loaf, tells the story of a mentally ill, unnamed narrator played by Norton who meets a chaotic, egotistical, philosophical, enigmatic man named Tyler Durden, played by Pitt. The two meet on a plane, striking a friendship along with a line of "fight clubs," where men meet to fight each other to blow off steam. The David Fincher film, based on a book by Chuck Palahniuk, follows the narrator as he moves in with Durden following the destruction of his apartment, which was destroyed in a fire caused by a blown out pilot light. Durden and the narrator live in squalor, their clothes constantly covered in the blood of the men they fight, always sporting bruises on their faces from a fight the night before. We are given clues to the conclusion of *Fight Club* mostly through the narrator's interactions with Helena Bonham Carter's character Marla Singer, who the narrator meets in the self-help groups he attends. Singer is then seen having sex with Tyler Durden. Their rampant sex sprees keep Norton's character up at night. We never see Durden, the narrator, and Singer in the same room. When the narrator and Singer are in the same room, he is short and cold with her. When Durden and the narrator are in the same room, Durden orders the narrator to not mention him to Singer. At one point, Singer says to the narrator, "You are such a nutcase, I can't begin to keep up." At that point, we don't fully understand why Singer would say that. We follow the narrator and Durden as they host the fight clubs, which become popular across the country.

Soon, the fight clubs turn into something else, something more sinister and anarchistic, which Durden and the narrator refer to as "Project Mayhem." Fighters show up to Durden and the narrator's dilapidated house on the outskirts of the city. The house is filled with men who are planning total societal destruction. At this point, the narrator feels like he's in the dark about the whole thing, with Durden leading the charge. "Tyler built himself an army," Norton says.

The police start to catch on to "Project Mayhem" when the men start a four-alarm fire in the shape of a smiley face in an apartment building. The narrator is shocked, saying that they've gone too far. The men do not listen. They are dedicated to the cause.

The film takes a turn when Durden, the narrator, and two of their men are in a car with Durden driving. Durden admits to the narrator that he was the one who blew up his apartment. He lets go of the steering wheel as they are on the highway, saying, "Stop trying to control everything and just let go." The car swerves back and forth across the highway until they crash and lose consciousness. When the narrator comes to, Durden is nowhere to be found.

This climax sets off the rest of the film as complete chaos ensues. The narrator finds plane tickets assigned to Tyler Durden and he proceeds to visit each of the cities in an attempt to find him. "Was I asleep? Had I slept? I was living in a perpetual state of déjà vu. I was always one step behind Tyler," the narrator says.

In one city, he goes to a bar and meets the bartender, who is beaten to a pulp with a brace surrounding his head, a clear participant in the fight clubs. He asks the bartender if he knows Durden, to which the man replies, "You're Mr. Durden." The twist is now apparent. Tyler Durden and the narrator are the same person. Durden is a figment of the narrator's imagination, an alter ego he created in all of his deep insanity.

When he turns himself into the police, the policemen are in on the plot. They are participants in the fight clubs, too. "Project Mayhem" was everywhere, it was inescapable. The narrator discovers that Durden's plot was to blow up all major bank buildings, resetting universal credit, bringing everyone back to zero, financially, putting everyone on the same playing field. The narrator flees the police and runs to an office building in the city to try to stop it from being blown up by those in "Project Mayhem." In the parking garage of the building, he sees a van and Durden appears. He and Durden fight each other, but now, we see through camera footage that the narrator is really just fighting himself. He gets knocked out and wakes up again in the office building, where Durden has a gun in his mouth. The narrator realizes, however, that because Durden is really just a personality he's created in his mind, he actually has the gun cocked in his own mouth. After a moment of contemplation, he thinks that the only way to get rid of Durden is to shoot himself. He does so, and Durden dies. The narrator is stuck with a massive bullet wound to his face. He is still alive. A few men from "Project Mayhem" arrive with Marla Singer, and the film ends with the narrator and Singer standing in the office space, holding hands as they watch the buildings in the city explode. "You met me at a very strange time in my life," the narrator tells Singer, the final line in the movie before the couple is blown to smithereens.

"As most of *Fight Club* didn't happen at all as the Narrator had told it, the ending becomes even more ambiguous. However, taken at face value, it shows that the Narrator is finally free of Brad Pitt's Tyler Durden, but that he can't stop Project Mayhem's plan, and so he simply watches it unfold," writes ScreenRant's Niall Gray in 2022. "The implications of this are that Project Mayhem's other groups across the globe will likely succeed in their mission, too, dealing a serious blow to the consumerist society that Tyler was rebelling against."

Gray continues to write about the themes of anti-consumerism and toxic masculinity which comes to light through the narrator's creation of Tyler Durden in his mind:

> One of *Fight Club*'s most obvious themes is that of anti-consumerism and its incompatibility with modern society. This is at the forefront of the film's story, with a number of Tyler's monologues delivered on exactly that subject. However, this is used as a front for the Narrator's deeper-seated issues, with Tyler using them as a smokescreen to distract him from his own mental state.
>
> The Narrator's creation of Tyler is representative of his struggle with his own masculinity. Tyler embodies all the qualities the Narrator wishes he had and is seemingly free of any inhibitions—something that the Narrator continues to struggle with

after Tyler's introduction. This is evidenced in the senseless violence and eventual terrorism that Tyler inspires in others, and its something that the Narrator protests. Tyler embodies toxic masculinity masquerading as a replacement for true therapy, as evidenced by his treatment of Marla and the way he physically manifests to the Narrator.

Shutter Island, based on a 2003 book by Dennis Lehane, is the fourth collaboration between Leonardo DiCaprio and Martin Scorsese, who worked together on *Gangs of New York*, *The Aviator*, and *The Departed* before embarking on the mystery thriller that would rake in $295 million at the box office when it was released in 2010 on an $80 million budget. The film would be a success at cineplexes around the world, becoming Scorsese's second-highest-grossing film worldwide. The film included a star-studded cast, which featured DiCaprio, Mark Ruffalo, Ben Kingsley, Michelle Williams, and Emily Mortimer, and a twist ending that would rival *The Sixth Sense* and *Fight Club*.

The storyline features Leonardo DiCaprio playing a US Marshal alongside his partner, Chuck Aule, played by Ruffalo. The two are assigned a case at Ashcliffe, the psychiatric hospital housing the criminally insane on an island in the middle of Boston Harbor, known as "Shutter Island." The movie was filmed in multiple locations around Massachusetts, with Peddocks Island being the central setting for the island, Nahant for the lighthouse scenes, and the Wilson Mountain Reservation in Dedham for the shots of the duo braving a strong hurricane.

Teddy Daniels (played by DiCaprio) and his partner, Aule, are headed to the island in search of a missing prisoner, Rachel Solando, played by Mortimer. Solando is imprisoned in the psychiatric facility for the criminally insane after she murdered her three children, drowning them in a lake. Daniels and Aule are welcomed by Dr. John Cawley, played by Kingsley, and Dr. Jeremiah Naehring, one of the doctors on the premises, played by Max von Sydow. The federal agents are determined to find Solando, who escaped the ward one night and is suspected to be wandering and hiding on the island from the orderlies and doctors. They interview many of the doctors and fellow patients to get an idea of how Solando spent her days leading up to the disappearance. According to the orderlies and patients, she acted mostly normal before she snuck out of the ward. There was no indication that she was about to bolt. While interviewing one of the orderlies, he confessed that he went to the bathroom during his shift. Solando must have escaped then.

As the US Marshals investigate, we see Daniels have flashbacks to his time in World War II, seeing dead bodies in the snow in Germany, along with flashbacks of his relationship with his dead wife, Dolores Chanal, played by Michelle Williams. When Daniels opens up to his partner, Chuck Aule, he says that Williams died in a fire set by a man named Andrew Laeddis, who he claims is a patient at Ashcliffe. When given this case, Daniels had ulterior motives for taking it. He wants to meet Laeddis, the man who supposedly killed his wife and children.

Soon, there is a hurricane that hits the island, causing the power to go out. When the backup generators also shut down, the doors to the patients' rooms are opened, leading them to roam the island free. At this point, Daniels believes that the doctors at Ashcliffe are participating in human experimentation with lobotomies and other harmful procedures being conducted on people like Rachel Solando. In Daniels' head, he wonders if Solando is made up. He is wrong. Dr. Cawley approaches Daniels, saying that they had found Solando wandering the island, and now she's back in her room. When he questions her, she thinks that Daniels is her dead husband, Jim. Daniels realizes that Solando is indeed a sick person and leaves her, developing a killer migraine in the process. That night, he has flash-backs of a little girl, dead in the snow.

"Why didn't you save me?" the girl asks Daniels. His dead wife appears in the dream with wet hair once more. "Why are you all wet?" Daniels asks her. She tells Daniels that Laeddis is still at Ward C in Ashcliffe, adding that the US Marshal must find him and kill him for vengeance.

The next day, Daniels makes his way to Ward C to find Laeddis. Instead of finding Laeddis, he finds a man named George Noyce, who has extensive facial scarring and tries to tell Daniels to not trust his partner, Chuck Aule. "This is a game. All this is for you," Noyce cryptically tells Daniels. The meeting is a vague setup for the major plot twist which turns the film into a mind-bending thriller with Scorsese at the helm.

Teddy Daniels decides to flee the hospital and head for the light-house, where he's sure that he will get answers. Along the way, he finds a cave where the *real* Rachel Solando is hiding. Solando number 2, played by Patricia Clarkson, tells Daniels that she used to be a doctor at Ashcliffe before she went mad and they made her a patient there. She says that Daniels faces the same fate. He will be deemed crazy by the doctors and will never be able to leave the island. Daniels is stunned, sleeping the night there with Solando before retreating in the morning. "You don't have a partner. You came here alone," she tells Daniels, another clue for what's to come.

Daniels heads back to Ashcliffe in the morning and decides to blow up Dr. Cawley's car. As he's running away to evade the blast, he sees his dead wife, Dolores and his dead daughter standing in front of the car, another hallucination. Daniels then escapes to the lighthouse, where the final twist happens to knock the viewer off their seat.

At the top of the lighthouse, Daniels breaks down a door to see Dr. Cawley sitting at a table. The doctor has been waiting for him to arrive and decides that now is the time to tell Daniels what's really happening on the island. He tells Daniels that the US Marshal had been a patient at Ashcliffe for two years. His name, Teddy Daniels, is an anagram for Anthony Laeddis and Dolores Chanal, his wife, is an anagram for Rachel Solando. Daniels is really Laeddis, and his dead wife, Chanal, is an anagram for Rachel Solando. Dolores killed Laeddis's three children, drowning them in a lake, before Laeddis kills his wife, shooting her in the stomach. Laeddis was a US Marshal back in the day, and since he's arrived at Ashcliffe, he developed an elaborate hallucination in which he was still working for the government, under the pseudonym Teddy Daniels. Daniels/Laeddis asks Dr. Cawley about his partner, Chuck Aule, and just as he does, Mark Ruffalo's character comes in the door in a suit. Dr. Cawley says that Aule is actually his therapist, Dr. Sheehan, whom he's been seeing for the last two years. For the last few weeks, the doctors and the orderlies have been playing into Daniels/Laeddis's delusion to see if it might make him realize the truth: he's been a patient at Ashcliffe this whole time. If Daniels/Laeddis can accept that he's a patient and not a US Marshal, he might be able to avoid being lobotomized. If not, they will go ahead with the procedure.

"I need to know you've accepted reality," Dr. Cawley says.

At first, Daniels/Laeddis confesses, tearfully, that yes, he did kill his wife after she killed their three children. However, in the last scene of the movie, he is sitting with Aule/Dr. Sheehan and says, "We're going to get off this rock, go to the mainland. Which is worse? To die as a monster or to live like a good man?" Daniels/Laeddis goes back into his delusion, and after doing so, Aule/Dr. Sheehan makes eye contact with Dr. Cawley, shaking his head, an indication that Daniels/Laeddis is back into his delusion. We are left wondering, did Daniels/Laeddis end up getting lobotomized? Was Rachel Solando truly made up, even though the US Marshal met her in the cave? How much of the story is a hallucination?

Roger Ebert writes in 2010:

> You may read reviews of *Shutter Island* complaining that the
> ending blindsides you. The uncertainty it causes prevents the
> film from feeling perfect on first viewing. I have a feeling it might
> improve on second. Some may believe it doesn't make sense. Or
> that, if it does, then the movie leading up to it doesn't. I asked
> myself: OK, then, how should it end? What would be more sat-
> isfactory? Why can't I be one of those critics who informs the
> director what he should have done instead?
>
> Oh, I've had moments like that. Every moviegoer does. But
> not with *Shutter Island*. This movie is all of a piece, even the
> parts that don't appear to fit. There is a human tendency to note
> carefully what goes before, and draw logical conclusions. But—
> what if you can't nail down exactly what went before? What if
> there were things about Cawley and his peculiar staff that were
> hidden? What if the movie lacks a reliable narrator? What if its
> point of view isn't omniscient but fragmented? Where can it all
> lead? What does it mean? We ask, and Teddy asks, too.

Shutter Island is one of those movies that lends itself to a second
and third watch to try to make sense of the ending. Like *The Sixth
Sense*, we are left wondering, "What did I miss? What is reality and
what is a hallucination?" and at that point of questioning the reality
in the story, we are urged to try to make sense of the twisted plot. We
are never given follow-up interviews from Scorsese and DiCaprio, or
even the book's author Dennis Lehane about the fate of the protagonist, leaving the ending up in the air for viewers.

In 2020, Indiewire's Zack Sharf writes:

> DiCaprio and Scorsese dropped this line of dialogue in *Shutter
> Island*: "Which would be worse: To live as a monster, or to die as
> a good man?" The line is asked by Andrew/Teddy, and in doing

so Scorsese and screenwriter Laeta Kalogridis leave the door somewhat open as to whether or not Andrew/Teddy is committing himself to a lobotomy in order to wash his mind from the sins of his past. It's an integral tweak from Lehane's book, which ends more conclusively as Andrew slips back into his Teddy persona. The question Andrew/Teddy asks in the film makes it a possibility that the character has become more sane and is making an active choice. If Andrew is sane, then committing himself to a lobotomy because he can't deal with the monster he's become turns *Shutter Island* into a haunting tragedy.

8

Is There Really a Sixth Sense?

Psychics, clairvoyants, witches, warlocks, spiritualists . . . all of these labels have been thrown around for generations since the early days of the Salem Witch Trials in the seventeenth century, but only for the last century have we seen such people in pop culture, particularly in film and television. Going back to the 1960s to 1970s with the sitcom *Bewitched*, starring Elizabeth Montgomery and Dick York, psychic powers were seen as fake and too otherworldly to be believable, but the concept still was intriguing to viewers.

In each episode, main character Samantha grapples with her abilities, making things move or disappear with her "sixth sense" that she activates through a twitch of the nose. Her husband, Darrin, wants her to relinquish and neglect her abilities, while her mother, Endora, wants her to stay true to her gifts and use them. In the seventeenth century, Samantha would have been burned at the stake. In the mid-twentieth century, however, viewers bit and the show was beloved. Samantha's daily life was comical and spooky. The show ran for eight seasons.

I Dream of Jeannie was another television hit during the late sixties which showcased a woman with powers to grant wishes. A little different than *Bewitched*, this woman was more alien, coming straight from a bottle like the genie we see in Disney's *Aladdin*. The interest in the supernatural spans generations, with mostly women being able to share their gifts like the witches who were burned in the Salem Witch Trials. Men with these gifts were rarely seen in the early days of television, until *Buffy the Vampire Slayer* featured characters Angel and Spike who were warlocks with magical powers to use for harm or for good. It took awhile for film and television to show men in these types of roles. Women were seen as ethereal while men were stoic and workhorses, tied to the material world rather than spiritually driven.

Becoming popular around the same time as *Buffy*, *Sabrina the Teenage Witch* with Melissa Joan Hart told another tale of a woman with supernatural powers, living with her female guardians and trying to live a "normal" life despite coming from a long line of witches. *Buffy* and *Sabrina* aired during the 1990s just before *The Sixth Sense* came out. They would both go on to receive Kid's Choice Awards in the late nineties. By this point, we rarely see men on television or in film who possess the same psychic gifts that women do. Witches and clairvoyants seemed to be reserved for those who identify as female, making Haley Joel Osment in *The Sixth Sense* a rare breed in pop culture.

The X-Files, which aired during the 1990s and wrapped up in 2002, also made waves on the small screen, an episodic series dealing with a different spooky story each episode. David Duchovny and Gillian Anderson play two FBI agents working in the "X-Files" division of the organization, a niche that deals with paranormal occurrences. Duchovny's Fox Mulder is a die-hard believer in all things paranormal while Gillian Anderson's Dana Scully serves as a skeptic looking for any and all logical explanations to explain the crazy cases they try to crack.

In one particular episode titled "Eve," which aired December 10, 1993, Mulder and Scully investigate the ritualistic killings of adults who have daughters who look exactly the same but live across the country from each other. By the end of the episode, we learn that a female doctor had been inseminating families with her DNA, creating a race of psychically gifted clones. We see two young female twins engaging in homicidal behavior and supernatural strength, one of the first instances of child paranormal abilities that we encounter in pop culture, specifically on the small screen.

Of course, paranormal abilities in children have been seen in other areas of media, including the 1976 film *The Omen*, where Damien, a young boy, is said to be the spawn of Satan, wreaking havoc in his parents' home. He possesses super strength and the ability to convince his babysitter to kill herself in an early scene in the film. From that point on, his mother realizes that the child is evil and homicidal while also possessing psychic and clairvoyant abilities.

And then there's the Stanley Kubrick classic *The Shining* released in 1980, based on Stephen King's book by the same title. In this, a young boy named Danny Torrance has a "sixth sense" that is referred to as "shining" where he can see the dead and predict the future. This is an early example of kids in pop culture being sensitive to otherworldly gifts and powers. Trapped in a hotel with his psychotic father and terrified mother, Danny starts seeing twin girls around the hotel asking for him to "Come play" with them. These girls, we learn later, were in fact ghosts killed by their father in a brutal ax-slaying. Caretaker Dick Hallorann, played by Scatman Crothers, immediately recognizes Danny as having what he refers to as "The Shining," because he, himself, has this power, too.

King also wrote *Firestarter* in 1980 about a young girl who has the ability to set things ablaze with her supernatural powers. The book was turned into a film by the same name, with a young Drew Barrymore playing Charlie, the psychically gifted daughter of parents who also possess psychic powers.

Carrie is yet another example of King writing about children with psychic abilities. The main character by the same name is mercilessly bullied at school. As the film progresses, we see that Carrie is telekinetic, able to move inanimate objects on her own. In a climactic scene where her bullies douse her in pig's blood at a school dance, Carrie fights back, setting the school gym on fire. The 1976 film starring a young Sissy Spacek is a cult favorite, sparking reboots in 2002 and 2013. The 2013 remake, starring Chloe Grace Moretz and Julianne Moore, received mixed reviews.

In the late 1990s, just before *The Sixth Sense* came out, a Disney Channel Original movie called *Halloweentown* also showed kids with psychic abilities, revolving around a teenage witch, much like Sabrina, named Marnie. In the film, she discovers that she is from a long line of witches, her grandmother living in a world where it is always Halloween. The grandmother visits her grandchildren on Halloween, and on this particular day, Marnie discovers that she has true powers as a young witch. She follows her grandmother to Halloweentown, where the location has been taken over by an evil warlock set to destroy the town. The young Marnie, played by Kimberly J. Brown, ventures to Halloweentown to help defeat the villain, who ends up being her biological father at the end of the film.

In 1994, a USA Today CNN Gallup Poll revealed that 70 million Americans believed it was possible to speak with the dead. Film, television, and perhaps their own personal experiences, led the American population to believe in the paranormal even before *The Sixth Sense* made waves at the box office.

And then, *The Sixth Sense* hit theaters. The main character, a young boy named Cole, can see the dead. Typically, with perhaps the exception of Damien in *The Omen* and Danny Torrance in *The Shining*, young girls and women are the ones with psychic gifts, but this time, a young, white, cisgendered boy is the star of the show, possessing clairvoyant abilities. Although we have seen the paranormal in film and television for decades, Shyamalan veered away from witches and warlocks and focused instead on a seemingly normal young boy with psychic gifts who could see and speak with the dead.

In October 1999, *People* magazine released a cover story, with the front page saying, "A hit movie has people asking: Is there a Sixth Sense? Whether they're mediums with a message or phonies after a fast buck, a new breed of psychic has made believers of millions who long to talk to the dead."

The article follows multiple professionals who offer psychic services to help clients talk to deceased family members. One is named George Anderson, who at the time of the article, was offering $400 sessions to clients. In a scene written by *People* magazine, Anderson rightly guesses that he is communicating with a couple's dead son who killed himself. He then rightly guesses that the father prays for the son "on the sly, quietly." The father nods in agreement, saying, "Yes, I know exactly what you mean."

"Whether you believe in ghosts or think those who do aren't playing with a full tarot deck, a lot of people these days seem to know—or want to know—exactly what Anderson means. For millions of Americans, mediums are the message they can't get enough of," *People* writes. "At the movies, the surprising success of *The Sixth Sense*, the eerie story of a boy with a megacase of ESP and the therapist who helps him come to terms with it, reflects a resurgence of fascination with things otherworldly."

According to *People*, books about contacting the dead had made their way onto the *New York Times* bestseller list in the years leading up to *The Sixth Sense*. Shows such as *Leeza*, *Montel*, and *Larry King Live* had been featuring segments on the paranormal.

Some psychics are legit while others scam you out of hundreds of dollars just to tell you that your loved one is at peace on the other side. Around the late 1990s, a Queens, New York, medium by the name of James Van Praagh was seeing celebrity clients such as Cher, who claimed that the psychic connected her to her late husband, Sonny Bono, who told her that he "watched his whole funeral and loved Cher's sentiments, but he does not like where he is buried."

Van Praagh told *People* magazine that "in two or three years, you're going to see more shows on mediums. More people are accepting it and buying into it."

Like a true psychic, he was right.

In 2003, Disney Channel released the kid's show *That's So Raven* which followed the main character, played by Raven Symoné, who could predict the future. And then, in 2005, NBC aired a show called *Medium* starring Patricia Arquette about a medium who worked with the local district attorney's office to crack cases based on psychic visions she would have about the crimes in question. *The Dead Zone* and *Psych*, both also released in the early 2000s, delved into the issue of psychic abilities, the former based on a novel by Stephen King.

And then, the reality shows about mediumship started. In 2011, the Travel Channel released a reality television series called *The Dead Files* and in the same year, TLC released *Long Island Medium*.

The premise of *The Dead Files* is this: medium Amy Allan and retired NYPD officer Steve DiSchiavi work on one paranormal case per episode. The cases range anywhere from poltergeist hauntings to demonic possessions of particular households across the United States. DiSchiavi is in charge of researching the history of the home in question while Amy heads out to investigate locations with no prior knowledge of the paranormal occurrences or history of the home. Each episode follows Amy's visions that she has at the homes and DiSchiavi's research at local libraries or speaking to people in the neighborhood for firsthand encounters and historical knowledge. In the last half hour of the episode, Amy and Steve meet with the people experiencing the hauntings to go over what they found. Often, Amy's psychic visions would directly relate to what Steve found while researching the house's history. To the skeptic, they might view this as just a scripted television series with no reality behind Amy's visions. To the believer, *The Dead Files* is not only accurate, but mind-blowing. Most of the episodes are left with Amy and Steve declaring that the residents of the haunted location should leave before anything gets worse. The two usually suggest that the homeowners contact a priest or priestess to cleanse the environment, but, if Amy and Steve believe that there is something demonic in the house, they should vacate immediately. The show is still running to this day.

Long Island Medium is another reality show about mediumship that started in 2011 and ended in 2019. Theresa Caputo, the Long Island Medium, claims that she can speak with the dead. Each episode follows the mother of two as she balances parenting with helping clients communicate with their deceased loved ones. A firecracker with a thick Long Island accent and huge blonde hair, Caputo was a lovable and believable medium, sharing accurate insights with the average person looking for answers. Since she left the show in 2019, she wrote a book called *Good Mourning* which helps readers through their grief. She also does group readings or one-on-one readings which currently have a waiting list. She charges anywhere from $50 to $175 a session.

The most recent mediumship reality tv show is hosted by Tyler Henry, a twenty-year-old self-proclaimed medium. The show, started in 2016, is called *Hollywood Medium with Tyler Henry*. In each episode, Henry meets with celebrities to help them connect with deceased loved ones and offers them advice for their lives based on his visions.

In 2018, Henry met with television personality Khloe Kardashian. During their meeting, Henry alluded to some relationship problems that Khloe would have in the future. He said that her life, in his visions, seemed to be more focused on career than romance, and that she was dealing with someone who was at a long distance from her. He was, of course, alluding to Khloe's then-NBA player partner Tristan Thompson. In 2019, the couple split. They are to this day entangled in a complicated relationship with Thompson regularly cheating on the Kardashian sister despite them having children together. Henry's clip went viral, with fans suggesting that Henry rightly predicted her split.

Then, in 2022, Henry met with Kris Jenner, with Khloe behind the scenes watching the meeting play out. During the session, Henry spat out facts that he would not have otherwise known, baffling the momager. He knew that her late husband, lawyer Robert Kardashian, had a special bond with a "monkey," which Kris and Khloe said must have been in reference to his childhood stuffed animal monkey, which Khloe still has. Henry also saw a vision of "windows," which Kris said must be in regard to a recent conversation Kris and Khloe had about switching out certain windows in the house just days before meeting Henry. He connected to Kris Jenner's biological father and stepfather, who both died in car accidents, and Robert Kardashian, Kris's late husband.

On a zoom call with Tamron Hall for her talk show in March 2022, Henry told the host that he first realized he had a gift when he was ten years old, a similar age to that of Cole Sear in *The Sixth Sense*. Henry, like Cole Sear, is a timid, blonde-haired, thin boy, looking almost exactly like an older Cole Sear. The similarities are uncanny. Henry said that he realized he was gifted when he was laying in bed one night and had an intuitive feeling that his grandmother was going to die. Die, she did, almost to the second of Henry having this feeling.

> I woke up one night and had what could only be described as a "knowingness" that my grandmother was going to die. It was the most bizarre thing. It felt like a memory that hadn't happened yet and it was really confusing, especially being only 10 [years old]. So I went into a room to try to explain this to my mom. I was upset. As we were talking, her phone rang and we

were interrupted. She told me to hold on, picked up the phone, and as she did, it was my dad calling her to tell her that he had just watched my grandmother die in front of him. So, that was really the catalyst, but at 10 years old, you don't recognize that as an ability. It's really just something that happened to me.

Hall then brought up Henry's session with late actor Alan Thicke, where he told the Canadian star that he should watch his heart health. Shortly thereafter, Thicke died from heart complications.

"Alan Thicke passed away in 2016. He was a guest on your show, and you told him to be mindful of his heart health," Hall said. "And then he passed away of heart complications and there were people who said, 'well, you just guessed, right? What are the odds? A man of a certain age, heart condition. . . .' How do you respond to moments like that?"

"I'll be the world's best guesser," Henry replied. "I always say, with the readings that I do, the emphasis is on validation, specifics that are unknowable. Whether I'm reading a celebrity or an every day person, I have to be able to come up with information that can't be Googled, can't be researched, can't be guessed, can't be gleaned from body language. By my client's own testaments, they often acknowledge those types of things come through."

He continued to explain that the visions come through, for him, as "active daydreams." He compares it to being in class with a teacher delivering a lesson and him drifting off into his daydreams, where he is able to tune into his intuition rather than logic.

"I happen to have the ability that when I sit with people, I get very strong intuitive impressions," Henry explained to Hall. "I don't see dead people walking around, it's not like *The Sixth Sense*, that would be terrifying. If anything, I kind of just train myself to get into an altered state of mind where I'm just hyper-receptive to anything that might pop into my head."

In 2001 and again in 2005, Gallup polled a subset of Americans to see what they thought about the paranormal. In an article released in June 2005, Gallup found that three in four Americans believe in the paranormal. 41 percent of Americans believe in ESP while 37 percent believe in haunted houses, the highest percentages found when subjects were polled. 21 percent believed that people could see and speak with the dead.

In 2001, two years after *The Sixth Sense* was released, 50 percent of people believed in ESP or extrasensory perception, with 27 percent not believing in the phenomenon. More than half the population also believed that the mind may be able to heal the body. Thirty-two percent believed, in 2001, in clairvoyance, and even less, 26 percent, believed this in a follow up poll in 2005. Twenty-eight percent of people, in 2001, thought that people had the capacity to speak with the dead. Even less, 21 percent, believed in the phenomena later in 2005.

Rosalyn Bruyere, a well-known energy healer, clairvoyant, and medicine woman who has helped Martin Scorsese, Barbra Streisand, James Coburn, and Cher, has spent the majority of her life dedicated to unorthodox healing practices, teaching courses on topics such as Ancient Egyptian healing techniques and chakra work, and researching child health. She says that she met a few children while working at the Kennedy Krieger Institute in Baltimore researching "The Value of Touch Healing for Critically and Chronically Ill Children" who possessed powers similar to Tyler Henry and Haley Joel Osment's character in *The Sixth Sense*.

Bruyere said:

> [The kids I worked with] were all diagnosed as perhaps having multiple personality disorder. And because I could see their aura, I could see the dissociative parts of them and could draw a picture of it for the psychiatrist that was treating them. And

there were two different children there that would occasionally say something about me that I knew that child had no way of knowing about me. It was just their perception of me. So yes, I thought, awesome. For two of them to have that ability was a big statistic.

She went on to describe her own abilities and cited occasions where she would enter a historic location in California's "missions," settled by Junipero Sera in the eighteenth century, where she would encounter spirits face-to-face.

We have 21 missions that are the foundations of California, and they go between San Diego and San Francisco. The original buildings are all there. And they're the oldest buildings in the state of California. This was long before there was an America that [Sera] started [founding] this. And so when you go into places like that, that are historical, I will occasionally see somebody that I think is a spirit and I'll get close to them. I don't want to startle them. I don't know what they're doing. You know, I just want to see if I can say hello or something. But I never know until I'm actually in conversation with them, when they lived. I know that they're gone. But did they live in 1754? Or did they live in 1822?

All of these are Franciscan churches. And the Franciscan robes look like Franciscan robes, whether they're from 1704, or whether they're from 1930. People get confused because they can't be open minded, and open minded is not what everybody thinks it is, it's not accepting things that you didn't accept before. It's accepting a view of time that you never accepted. For almost everyone, time is very fixed, even now down to nanoseconds, and it goes in the straight line. But when you're on a historic site that has a history, you don't know when you're out there if you're talking with a relative of the battle, or one of the soldiers of a battle, or a Native American, whose territory those things were fought on. So you could be going back 400 years to a native village or something that was there before that became a battleground.

Bruyere believes that any exposure for clairvoyants is good exposure, stating that *The X-Files*, *The Sixth Sense*, and *Phenomena* with John Travolta have all been good representations of psychic and paranormal occurrences. She says that the only harmful depictions in pop culture are movies like *Firestarter* or *Carrie* which feature the protagonist using their abilities for evil. When it comes from a place of revenge or hate, Bruyere says that it is harmful and inaccurate from how life really is. People who have psychic powers aren't out for revenge or blood, they're just trying to live their lives as normally as possible.

Instead of shutting children away and deeming them insane, Bruyere believes that we should be asking them to share their experiences more and more in order to understand where they are coming from and how we can help. She adds:

> There's no question in my mind that children see this stuff. I mean, if you don't think children see that stuff, you have to wipe out most of British literature. Because there's all kinds of metaphysical stuff in just your reading list from a college English class. My question to that character, who would be standing in front of me, is, tell me more about how you see and what you see. I wouldn't question whether he saw it. He just told me did. Therefore, tell me what you see and how you see it.

The Sixth Sense undoubtedly sparked an interest in all things paranormal when it came out in the late 1990s. Yes, there were films and television shows released before Shyamalan's film which delved into the theory of mediumship and clairvoyance, but reality shows and films post–*The Sixth Sense* really took off and became part of mainstream culture, with *The Dead Files, Long Island Medium*, and *Hollywood Medium with Tyler Henry* making waves on cable television. Shyamalan found a way to convince viewers that mediumship is real, changing American culture forever.

9

Off-Screen Shenanigans

It wasn't all work and no play on the set of *The Sixth Sense*. Bruce Willis, a once popular musician back in the 1980s, liked to host DJ sets after hours for the cast and crew to let loose after hard days of filming, rehearsing, and watching dailies. Shyamalan recalled these sets being booze-fueled, with Willis playing popular songs for the rest of the folks to enjoy. There was dancing and drinking and the young filmmaker recalled that Willis gave Shyamalan his "first hangover." Prior to meeting Willis and attending these shindigs, Shyalaman hadn't been much of a drinker. He did not view this kind of fun as a priority. He was a hard worker, focused on making *The Sixth Sense* into an Oscar-nominated phenomenon. His parents were doctors, strict, wanting their son to prioritize his work over play. Willis knew how to have a good time, and he showed Shyamalan exactly what that meant when he hosted these after-hours parties.

"Bruce definitely introduced me to the notion of partying and letting loose," Shyamalan told me for an oral history of *The Sixth Sense*, released by *Variety* in 2019. "Back in those days, he was a big DJ and the parties were super fun. He definitely gave me my first hangover. He'd always keep giving me shots that he kept calling 'candy': 'Here's candy, here's candy.' And then the next morning I could not get off the sofa. And I didn't know what this throbbing pain in my head was. He was just laughing his butt off."

While Willis hosted parties after-hours, the kids of *The Sixth Sense* would play with each other in the large convention center with Mischa Barton often wandering off to explore the building.

"I do remember sneaking up to the rafters into the higher levels. It was kind of just dilapidated and not that great, but you could get a good vantage point over the steps from above. We'd go do that anyway, even though we were highly discouraged by anybody, any PA who could get their hands on us," Barton said.

The young actress, who would commute from New York to Philadelphia, stayed on set for two weeks even though she was only in a couple of scenes. While she was there, she said she was happy to have other young actors around like Osment and Trevor Morgan, who played Cole Sear's bully in the film. The kids played together and wandered around during their downtime, which Barton said she had a lot of. The camaraderie on the set of *The Sixth Sense* was just as present and meaningful for the kids as it was for the adults, who would party after hours with Willis deejaying.

"I was there for a lot longer than I needed to be. I had a lot of downtime. It was fun for me because I just liked the camaraderie of being on a set with kids my own age," Barton recalled. "We used to play racquetball in the hallway. Haley used to like to play with his tennis ball in the hallway to blow off steam and that was fun."

Barton, who worked on another film with Bruce Willis called *Assassination of a High School President* in 2008, said that Willis would spend time with the kids on *The Sixth Sense* set, bringing some joy and laughter to their days, making the set of the film a comfortable one for children to work on.

"Bruce was really sweet with us. Whenever he could find the kids he would always entertain us briefly. He was always very happy and goofy. I've actually done another movie with Bruce and it was different on that set. He was always just in his trailer playing music. But on this set [*The Sixth Sense*] he was always quite engaging."

The cast and crew of *The Sixth Sense* made time for fun while on set at the Philadelphia Convention Center, with Willis and Shyamalan creating a friendly environment for the rest of those involved in the picture. At the end of the day, the set was as fun-loving as it was productive for everyone involved.

10

Did They Know It Would Succeed?

When Haley Joel Osment, Toni Collette, and Bruce Willis read Shyamalan's script for *The Sixth Sense*, they knew that the material was strong, but no one, not even now defunct Hollywood Pictures who produced the film, had any idea that the summer hit would become the second-most successful film at the box office in 1999. Opening five weeks before Labor Day weekend in 1999, it held the number one spot and continued to succeed until the holiday, raking in $26 million, $25 million, $23 million, $20 million, and finally $29 million over Labor Day weekend. The only film that beat out *The Sixth Sense* in 1999 was *Star Wars Episode I: The Phantom Menace* which was released in May, a few months before Shyamalan's horror-drama. Looking back on the year as a whole, *The Sixth Sense* made more money than *Toy Story 2*, *The Matrix*, *The Blair Witch Project*, and Oscar-winning best picture of the year *American Beauty* with Kevin Spacey and Annette Bening. Although the actors and crew knew they had something special, they were not prepared for the overwhelmingly positive critical reception of the film and its money-making ability in comparison to the other hugely successful films just before the turn of the twenty-first century. Its success, largely, is because of positive word-of-mouth for the twist ending that would shock everyone watching.

"The story of *The Sixth Sense*'s word-of-mouth triumph is the kind of industry narrative studios still salivate over but used to build their entire financial operations around," notes staff writer David Sims of the *Atlantic* in "How *The Sixth Sense* Conquered Hollywood in 1999" in August 2019. "Yes, not every mid-budgeted genre picture is going to be a runaway hit, and not every August release will be remembered past its opening weekend. But once in a while, there will be a flabbergasting, market-correcting phenomenon that few could have predicted, one that justifies production companies sinking tens of millions into films that aren't guaranteed moneymakers."

In fact, Hollywood Pictures did sink $40,000,000 into the picture, which at the time was miniscule compared to Twentieth Century Fox's budget of $115,000,000 for *Star Wars Episode I: The Phantom Menace*, but much larger than DreamWorks' budget for *American Beauty* at $15,000,000. The budget for *The Sixth Sense* is actually more comparable to another thriller released in 1999: *The Blair Witch Project*, a "found footage film" that paved the way for other films like the *Paranormal Activity* franchise with its mockumentary style. Shyamalan would even later hop on the found-footage bandwagon with *The Visit* in 2015. *The Blair Witch Project*, which followed three filmmakers in a hunt for the elusive and dangerous Blair Witch in West Virginia, cost just $20,000 more than *The Sixth Sense*. This is surprising because *The Blair Witch* looks like it barely cost anything at all to make. There seemed to be lower-grade cameras used and the production design rarely deviated from camp sites and wooded areas. Shyamalan's *Sixth Sense* required many set changes, crew members, and expensive cast members like Bruce Willis, and yet, it was cheaper to make than the found-footage films. What set Shyamalan's film apart from other flicks of 1999, Sims writes, is because of "the power of the twist."

"The power of the twist was twofold. It encouraged new viewers to see *The Sixth Sense* every week, as others spread word about the surprise ending, but it also spurred people to see the movie again with fresh eyes," Sims writes.

The twist ending set *The Sixth Sense* apart from all of the other films of 1999, with nearly every viewer feeling flabbergasted by the trick. The twist, luckily for Shyamalan and the studios, would be kept under wraps, with moviegoers respecting the secret. To this day, those who haven't seen the movie still have no idea that Dr. Crowe was dead the whole time. It is only until they watch the flick that they learn of this expertly crafted move by Shyamalan.

"We showed it to 1,000 people before it was known. 1,000 people came back and had no idea, just a collective gasp of 1,000 people," Shyamalan said in Kiselyak's documentary *The Sixth Sense: Reflections From the Set* in 2008. "That was the perfect scenario because they had no idea there was a twist ending. The place was stunned at the end, absolute silence, no clapping, nothing. Credits started rolling and there was this feeling of overwhelm, they were overwhelmed by what they just saw. It was a fun time."

Roth recalled the first viewing of *The Sixth Sense* as the turning point when he realized that the film was going to be groundbreaking. Sitting in the middle of the theater, the ex-chairman of Disney was hyper aware of the crowd's reactions. Typically, you see moviegoers leave their seats and head to get more snacks or go to the bathroom. He saw none of this. He was also aware of the audience's reaction to the plot twist at the end. He thought for sure that at least someone would guess the twist by the end of the picture, but no one did. Roth sensed the feeling of relief during the second to last scene where Osment and Collette finally talk about Cole's ability to see the dead. Shyamalan's film didn't stop there, however, and Roth recalls the collective gasp and uproar when the final scene played. Crowe's wedding ring rolled to the ground and the audience then realized, "Oh, my gosh. Dr. Crowe has been dead this whole time." Roth hadn't experienced anything like the first screening. After reading hundreds of scripts a year, *The Sixth Sense* stands out for him as being in the top five most influential movies he's been a part of.

"When we went to test the movie, I realized that if people figured out what the surprise was before the surprise, it would be terrible. There were 600 people in the audience and nobody moved. The surprise happens, and the place erupts. They don't even leave after the movie, they're talking about what had just happened."

Iconic critic Roger Ebert was equally stunned by the ending, leading him to write a rave review of the film when it came out in 1999.

"I have to admit I was blind-sided by the ending," Ebert writes. "The solution to many of the film's puzzlements is right there in plain view, and the movie hasn't cheated, but the very boldness of the storytelling carried me right past the crucial hints and right through to the end of the film, where everything takes on an intriguing new dimension."

Desson Howe of the *Washington Post* also praised Shyamalan in a 1999 review of the film, hailing the way that the writer/director developed the film into a climax that would shock every viewer in the room. He writes:

> Writer/director M. Night Shyamalan knows how to build atmosphere—this is clear. And he does it painstakingly, brick by brick. By the end of the picture, a very powerful design becomes clear, with a twist that will put your head in a swirl. And launch some spirited discussion, I'd hope. That final section—in which everything is "explained"—may not work for some people. Personally, I bought it hook, line and sinker because I was so connected to the drama by that point. That was thanks to subtle work from Bruce Willis, who plays a child psychologist, and a remarkable performance from Haley Joel Osment—as the child he tries to help.

During the filming process, Barton, Osment, Willis, and Collette were going through the motions without thinking too much about how the film would be received, going into dailies to see where they might need work to get their scenes in tip-top shape. Each day they would be critiqued by Shyamalan and the rest of the cast and crew, and even the scariest scenes, like Barton under the bed spewing vomit from her mouth, did not really faze the young or old cast members at the time. It was when the film was finally finished and started screening in front of the cast and crew members that they really understood the gravity of the performances and the success of the film as a whole.

"The first time I remember seeing a lot of it other than dailies was at Disney's lot in Burbank in the Seven Dwarves building where they had some screening rooms. I went there with my whole family except for my younger sister who was too young. A friend of mine came, and I remember him getting really scared by it. That was the first time I was like, 'Oh, wow, this is what this movie does to people,'" Osment said.

Barton had a similar experience when she watched the film go through ADR to improve the sound quality of certain scenes in a controlled setting. Barton brought her mother and sister with her, and her sister, even though she was supposed to be silent, screamed when Barton was shown under the bed and in Cole's tent spewing vomit.

Barton said:

> The first time we realized how intense and scary it was was when I went in to do ADR, and I actually had my little sister in the room because we went into this studio in New York to do the ADR and she just, like, literally flipped. You know how you're not supposed to make any noise in ADR? She screamed at the top of her lungs. My mom was like, "Oh, my God." She had to take her outside. My sister's like, "That's the scariest thing I've seen." I never went back to school as just a regular kid anymore.

All these kids went to the movie theater and they were like "Is that you?" The whole school treated me differently. I don't think the teachers knew what to do with me.

Barton reflected on the film, saying that it probably would not be the type of movie that would succeed if it were released today. In the age of the Internet, the ending would be spoiled very quickly. Luckily for the cast and crew, the secret twist was kept under wraps when it arrived in theaters and on VHS, surprising everyone who watched it and enticing viewers to go back and watch the film again and again.

[The Sixth Sense], I have to say, I still think is a great film. I still think it's an interesting film. It's a very cool storyline and it was before the age of spoilers, slightly. It was kind of nice that people were really shocked by the ending, something I'm not sure you could really get away with these days. It was a really great script. It was a very lucky ensemble cast, as well. I think everybody's great in it. I don't think you could make that movie now, anymore. I think [*The Sixth Sense*] is particularly special in [Night's] repertoire. I just don't think that scripts like that really hold as much gravitas anymore in terms of getting green-lit. It would have to be a really great director, like an Almodóvar (*Volver, Pain and Glory*), somebody who's really loved in order to get something like that greenlit because [*The Sixth Sense*] was a huge studio movie. I just don't think that's what studios are making at the moment, unless you have a fantastic director.

Barton, who was thirteen at the time, said that she was too young to realize how successful and groundbreaking *The Sixth Sense* was until she got a little older. Upon going back to school in New York City, kids did tease her about her role, but it wasn't until years later that she's really understood the impact that the film had on the movie industry and the paranormal genre in general.

Barton recalled:

> It wasn't until after it came out and everything [that I real-
> ized how successful the film was]. That's the blessing of being
> a young adult: the older you get, the more aware you are that
> this is supposed to be an Oscar worthy film. When you're a kid,
> you just don't know. You go in and you have fun, you do it and
> shoot out. I don't think that [being an Oscar worthy movie] was
> the expectation for this film. I mean, obviously there were huge
> actors, but I think Night did a good job of keeping it pretty mel-
> low on set, not like some sets I've been on where you have this
> really underlying kind of tension. This set felt more easy.

Word of mouth along with a family-friendly PG-13 rating caused
viewers to flock to what *Variety* called the Sleeper of the Summer for
initial viewing. After being shocked by the surprise ending, the same
viewers went back to their multiplexes to see *The Sixth Sense* a second time. Upon rewatching, they would find clues that Shyamalan
placed throughout the film to subtly hint at the fact that Dr. Crowe
was dead the whole time. For instance, Bruce never actually interacts
with anyone besides Cole Sear. Upon multiple watches, viewers see
that in the scenes where Cole, Lynn, and Dr. Crowe are together,
Lynn and Dr. Crowe never have actual direct communication with
one another. In a scene where Cole meets Dr. Crowe in his home,
the three characters are in the same room, but Lynn quickly asks
Cole if he wants a snack and then leaves. Later, in the hospital, Dr.
Crowe, Lynn, and Cole are speaking to the doctor about what may
be wrong with Cole, but Dr. Crowe never addresses the other doctor
directly and Lynn never speaks one-on-one or in a group with Willis's character.

Upon a rewatch, the viewer also notices that Willis is wearing the
same outfit the entire time: a buttoned up white shirt, slacks, and a

long trench coat. He also never speaks directly to his wife. He only spends time in his office when he is home, interacting with Olivia Williams's character only when she is sleeping on the couch. Whenever Dr. Crowe is present, people get cold, which is a historically telltale sign that ghosts are around. Dr. Crowe's wife's breath can be seen when Dr. Crowe is around her, speaking to her, and Lynn Sear at one point shudders and zips up her coat when Dr. Crowe is near her.

Also, Dr. Crowe does not wear his wedding ring. Whenever he writes in the film, Willis writes with his right hand to throw off viewers. Willis, who is left-handed, had to learn to write with his right hand for the part of Dr. Crowe. In the final scene, we see Dr. Crowe's wife drop a wedding ring on the ground, presumably her husbands. Dr. Crowe sees the ring on the ground, looks at his empty left ring finger, and the puzzle pieces start fitting into place for him. He realizes then that he is dead.

In a clever scene by Shyamalan, Dr. Crowe and his wife are celebrating their anniversary at a restaurant. Dr. Crowe shows up late and sits across from his wife, who seems aggravated by his tardiness. In reality, however, Dr. Crowe's wife is celebrating by herself, as her husband is dead. The bill comes for the food and Anna immediately takes the check and puts her card on file. Dr. Crowe is repetitively apologizing for being late, but Anna seems detached, aggravated, and giving him the silent treatment. When rewatching this scene, however, we realize that she is not aggravated with his absence; he's not even there to begin with. He's dead and she's left to celebrate their anniversary alone.

Around the same time that *The Sixth Sense* came out, other films like *Runaway Bride*, *The Blair Witch Project*, *The Thomas Crown Affair*, and *Mystery Men* were competing at the box office. Not one of those films could outdo Shyamalan's trippy thriller, which would bring in audiences of all ages, genders, and races. "If women and couples were going to *Runaway Bride*, the teens and hipsters to *Blair Witch* and the male action fans to *The Thomas Crown Affair* and *Mystery Men*, who would be left to see a film whose trailer tagline was an 8-year-old saying 'I see dead people?' The answer, in retrospect, seems obvious: Everyone," *Variety* box office reporter Ben Fritz wrote in 1999.

For Willis, the lead actor told journalist Charlie Rose that he believes the film succeeded because people didn't ruin the ending of the film to their friends and family, but instead let viewers experience the twist on their own.

"I think there's a lot of interest in the phenomenon of—you know, the idea of what happens after we die. The reason I think it was so successful financially is because people didn't tell their friends the ending of the film," Willis said. "And because we were so successful at fooling the audience, I think a lot of people went back a couple of times to see how they got fooled. It certainly was a phenomenal thing. It definitely made some money."

With its monumental success at the box office, Shyamalan and the crew started to think about potential Oscar nominations. Horror movies rarely get nominated at the Oscars, but *The Sixth Sense* was so much more than a horror flick like the low-budget *The Blair Witch Project*, which followed a group of young adults traipsing through the woods in Burkittsville, Maryland, to find the legendary Blair Witch, an entity said to inhabit the woods, much like the Mexican legend La Llorona and the Celtic Banshee myths, which say that grieving women, often witches, lure innocent victims to them to torture and kill by emitting a screaming crying throughout wooded areas. In *The Blair Witch Project* we see the three filmmakers encounter mysterious rock formations and stick figure dolls hanging at their campsites. We don't hear much noise from the Witch, but we do hear rustlings and footsteps by the tents. The film lacks in gore and does not ever show the Witch's form, leaving it up to the viewer to create an image of what the Witch might look like. The power of suggestion is what makes *The Blair Witch Project* truly effective, but it is no match for *The Sixth Sense*, a film with superb acting and a twist that would haunt viewers for decades. Shyamalan's efforts along with a stellar cast and crew put *The Sixth Sense* in the running for six Academy awards: Best Picture, Best Director, Best Supporting Actor, Best Supporting Actress, Best Original Screenplay, and Best Film Editing.

Haley Joel Osment would become the tenth youngest actor nominated for an Oscar, followed by Anna Paquin for the 1993 movie *The Piano*, Patty McCormack for the 1956 movie *The Bad Seed*, Abigail Breslin for the 2006 film *Little Miss Sunshine*, Quinn Cummings for the 1997 film *The Goodbye Girl*, Quvenzhané Wallis for the 2012 film *Beasts of the Southern Wild*, Mary Badham for the 1962 movie *To Kill a Mockingbird*, Tatum O'Neal for the 1973 film *Paper Moon*, Jackie Cooper for the 1931 film *Skippy*, and Justin Henry for the 1979 film *Kramer vs. Kramer*. At the Oscars, Osment ran against Tom Cruise in *Magnolia*, Jude Law in *The Talented Mr. Ripley*, Michael Caine in *The Cider House Rules* and Michael Clarke Duncan in *The Green Mile*. He would lose out to Michael Caine for the Academy Award race for best supporting actor.

"Haley, when I saw you, I thought, well that's me out of it. So, really, I'm basically up here to represent you guys as what I hope you will all be, a survivor," said Caine onstage at the Oscars.

Osment would be referenced in Billy Crystal's opening speech at the 2000 Academy Awards, where he sang and entertained the room of accomplished filmmakers and actors.

Crystal said:

> Another great story this year was *The Sixth Sense* and the success of the great young actor Haley Joel Osment who's sitting right over there. Hey, Haley! Welcome. 11 years old, God, I've had movies in development longer than that. Haley, this one's for you! People, kids who see dead people, are the spookiest

people in the world. You're 11, chatting with folks in heaven, so if you see my uncle Doug, tell him I didn't pull the plug. You see things that ain't there like Bruce Willis with hair. You're in *The Sixth Sense*, he was so great in *The Sixth Sense*. You may go home with Oscar and with Cher.

The young Osment recalled his experience at the Oscars with Christi Carras of the *Los Angeles Times* in a 2019 article, saying that during commercial breaks he was able to meet other actors who were nominated that night.

> The awards season is so crazy that it's sort of reassuring to see that most other people, who have had a lot more experience than I did at that age, are aware that it's a surreal experience and that there's no pressure that you have to be ready to handle this thing. I'd actually had my first meeting with Steven Spielberg at the end of 1999—so right as all of that was starting to heat up— and I remember him saying, "The best part about the Oscars is watching at the commercial breaks, when all these famous stars that you know are running around like audience members themselves trying to meet the people that they are enamored with," and that ended up being the case. Jude Law came over to my seat for the first time, and was like, "Hey, I heard we're play- ing robots in this movie with Steven Spielberg," and that was the first time we met.

Toni Collette was also nominated that night for her role in *The Sixth Sense* as Lynn Sear, Osment's on-screen mother. She ran against Angelina Jolie in *Girl, Interrupted*, Chloë Sevigny for *Boys Don't Cry*, Samantha Morton in *Sweet and Lowdown*, and Catherine Keener of *Being John Malkovich*. Jolie would beat Collette out for the statue, her first Oscar nomination and win. Jolie's character in *Girl, Interrupted*, Lisa Rowe, was a troublemaking badass psych ward patient who took

Winona Ryder's character Susanna Kaysen under her wing. The film was based on the book, *Girl, Interrupted*, by Susanna Kaysen, a true story about women getting help at a psychiatric hospital outside of Boston. Ryder, Jolie, and the late Brittany Murphy would be remembered for their roles in the film for years to come.

As for Best Director, M. Night Shyamalan was up against Michael Mann for *The Insider*, Lasse Hallstrom for *The Cider House Rules*, Spike Jonze for *Being John Malkovich*, and Sam Mendes for *American Beauty*. He was beaten out by Mendes the night of the Oscars, an Englishman who received the script for *American Beauty* from Steven Spielberg. *American Beauty* follows a dysfunctional American family trying to be happy despite living mediocre, boring lives. Kevin Spacey and Annette Bening play a married couple with a daughter, Jane Burnham, played by Thora Birch. Lester Burnham, played by Spacey, develops a crush on his daughter's high school friend Angela Hayes, played by Mena Suvari, while his daughter, Jane, develops feelings for her elusive next-door neighbor, played by Wes Bentley, who films everything, including Jane, without permission. In the first scene of the movie, we learn that it is Lester Burnham's last day on Earth, and for the rest of the film, we are left wondering what will happen to him. The complex storyline involving a cast of reputable actors and actresses blew critics and viewers away and would earn Mendes the Oscar for Best Direction and later, Best Picture.

Shyamalan was also nominated for Best Screenplay alongside Paul Thomas Anderson for *Magnolia*, Mike Leigh for *Topsy-Turvey*, Alan Ball for *American Beauty*, and Charlie Kaufman for *Being John Malkovich*. Ball won another statue for the crew of *American Beauty*.

For Best Film Editing, Andrew Mondshein was nominated for his work on *The Sixth Sense*; Zach Staenberg was nominated for *The Matrix*; Tariq Anwar and Christopher Greenbury were nominated for *American Beauty*; Lisa Zeno Churgin for *The Cider House Rules*; and William Goldenburg, Paul Rubell, and David Rosenblum for

The Insider. Staenburg won. *The Matrix*, a sci-fi thriller featuring Keanu Reeves, Lawrence Fishburne, Carrie-Ann Moss, and Hugo Weaving, tells the complicated story of a dystopian world in which we are living in a simulated reality. The film has lots of action scenes and instances of CGI, including perhaps the most memorable scene in which Reeves's character Neo dodges bullets by arching his back and waving his arms in slo-mo fashion, the bullets leaving a trail behind them as they are shot in Neo's direction. It is no wonder that *The Matrix* won for best film editing, as it is the most technically complicated of those movies nominated for the statue.

At the end of the day, *American Beauty* swept the 72nd annual Academy Awards, winning best picture, too. The other nominees included *The Sixth Sense*, *The Cider House Rules*, *The Insider*, and *The Green Mile*.

The Sixth Sense, although it did not sweep at the Oscars in 2000, raked in several awards at the People's Choice Awards in 2000. Shyamalan and the team won the People's Choice Award for Favorite Motion Picture Star in a Drama for Bruce Willis, Favorite Dramatic Movie, and Favorite Motion Picture. For Favorite Motion Picture, *The Sixth Sense* beat out *The Matrix* and *Star Wars Episode I: The Phantom Menace*. For Favorite Motion Picture Actor, Willis beat Harrison Ford and Mel Gibson. For Favorite Dramatic Movie, *The Sixth Sense* beat *Double Jeopardy* and *The Blair Witch Project*.

At the "MTV Movie Awards" in June of 2000, Haley Joel Osment won Best Male Breakthrough Performance, beating Michael Clarke Duncan, Wes Bentley, Jason Biggs, and Jamie Foxx for their performances. He called in from Poland, where he was on location for a film, thanking MTV for the award. *The Sixth Sense* was also nominated for Best Movie, Best Male Performance, and Best On-Screen Duo. Willis lost to Keanu Reeves for Best Male Performance and both Willis and Osment lost out to Verne Troyer and Mike Myers for their performance in *Austin Powers: The Spy Who Shagged Me.*

Troyer and Myers' onscreen chemistry for the James Bond spoof movie was hysterical and memorable as they played Mini Me and Dr. Evil, the villains of the Mike Myers–led film. Myers also played Fat Bastard and Austin Powers himself, switching characters with ease, talent, and most importantly, humor. The film isn't the first time Myers has played multiple characters as he also plays the lead role Stuart Mackenzie, as well as Stuart's Scottish father, in the 1993 comedy *So I Married an Ax Murderer*, about a man who believes he is dating a female serial killer, played by Nancy Travis. It's no surprise that Troyer and Myers won for best duo as the two inspired Halloween costumes for that year and years to come, becoming one of the most recognizable pop culture references of the late nineties.

The Sixth Sense also raked in at the Saturn Awards in early June for Best Horror Film and Best Young Actor/Actress for young Haley Joel Osment. The film was also nominated for Best Writing and Best Actor for Bruce Willis. Shyamalan would finally get recognized for his writing at the Satellite Awards in January 2000 when he won the award for Best Original Screenplay, at the Empire Awards for Best Director and at the Nebula Awards for Best Script. Andrew Mondshein would also win a Satellite Award for Best Film Editing. Collette would be nominated once again for her performance in *The Sixth Sense*, but would lose out to Chloë Sevigny for *Boys Don't Cry*.

Osment raked in awards at some of the lesser known events such as the Kansas City Film Critics Circle Awards, where he won Best Supporting Actor. He would shine again in January 2000 at the Las Vegas Film Critics Society Awards, where he swept the Best Supporting Actor, Most Promising Actor, and the Youth in Film Award. He was nominated for a Screen Actors Guild Award for Outstanding Performance by a Male Actor in a Supporting Role as well, but would lose out once more to Michael Caine for *The Cider House Rules*.

Writes Michael Rechtshaffen for the *Hollywood Reporter* in August 1999:

While Willis, Collette and Williams are fine, the film is handily stolen by 11-year-old Osment, probably best known as young Tom Hanks in *Forrest Gump* His soulful, sad-eyed performance provides the film with an affecting emotional center that helps offset Shyamalan's weakness for occasionally burdening scenes in weighty significance. But his decision to delay bringing out the bogeyman until well into the story, allowing the unsettling mood to build fully, is a refreshing change from the usual slice 'n' dice assault on the senses. Although there's sticky, New Age-y subtext to some of the plot resolutions, it's nice to see old-fashioned storytelling and staging serving as the picture's most potent special effects.

In a review written by Paul Clinton for CNN in 1999, the reviewer also praised Osment as a scene-stealer and the best part about *The Sixth Sense*, beating out Collette and Willis's performances even though they were veterans of the industry. He also hailed the twist ending, writing that the plot turn is, along with Osment's performance, why Shyamalan's sleeper summer flick is worth the watch. Clinton writes:

This is the second directorial effort by M. Night Shyamalan, who also wrote the script. For the most part, *The Sixth Sense* is crafted fairly well in terms of mood and production design. But ultimately it's a slow-moving story about the paranormal. It's also a lot less scary than it could be. But this film primarily is all about Osment, who gives an outstanding performance as the centerpiece of the movie. He's been acting since the age of 5 and audiences may remember him from five years ago when he appeared as the title character's son at the end of *Forrest Gump*. Without him, this film would be far less compelling. Willis turns in a measured and understated performance. And Toni Collette—who played the title role in the 1994 Australian film *Muriel's Wedding*—is believable as the boy's confused and frightened mother, although her character offers her a limited range of emotion. *The Sixth Sense* may be worth seeing for many, if only for its surprise ending. It's a finale that could make you think long and hard about death and an afterlife.

11

The Legacy of M. Night Shyamalan

When M. Night Shyamalan speaks about his legacy, whether it be in interviews with magazines or in commencement speeches for college graduates, he says that there are two ways to look at his career. In one version, he is a triumphant, revolutionary director and screenwriter, one of the highest paid in history. In another version, he is mediocre at best, turning out flop after flop, constantly eviscerated by critics for every creative project he churns out. There's one thing about his career that is undoubtedly true among critics and fans alike: *The Sixth Sense* was the highlight of his tenure as a filmmaker, with only the Mel Gibson-starring *Signs* coming in a close second.

Night deems himself as the "highest paid writer in the world," with dozens of screenplays under his belt. He's worked with A-Listers like Bruce Willis, Toni Collette, James McAvoy, Samuel L. Jackson, and Joaquin Phoenix. Many actors and crew members praise Shyamalan as being one of the most thorough and driven directors to work with because of his tenacity, focus, and preparation.

Looking back on Shyamalan's career, *Hollywood Insider*'s Sean Aversa writes in 2021:

> Night Shyamalan broke into Hollywood through the aforementioned *The Sixth Sense* that engaged and captivated audiences with its mysterious concept and spectacular twist. The element

of "the twist" is one that became a Shyamalan-staple moving forward into his career due to the success and genius of the ending of *The Sixth Sense*. This unexpected ending has garnered praise for its cleverness, but I don't often hear praise for Shyamalan taking the risk to completely alter the audience's perspective of the film in the closing moments of his film. In hindsight, there would never be a question as to whether the twist was right for the film—however in the development process of the film, it would have been easy to question oneself about such a deviation from conventional endings to a story, yet Shyamalan chose to be bold and to do something different.

All other films after *The Sixth Sense* would be afterthoughts. That's not to say that his films aren't good, they're just not up to the same caliber as the late nineties horror drama. Shyamalan would employ twist endings in films like *The Village* and *Devil* and sure, they're effective, but they were not nearly as monumental as *The Sixth Sense* was. And throughout the process of filming, cast and crew members praised Shyamalan's expertise, decisiveness, and playfulness while on set.

Haley Joel Osment, who worked with Night on *The Sixth Sense*, recalled how calm and peaceful Night was on set and how he treated the young boy like an adult, telling him, for instance, to not be sad when playing Cole Sear, but instead access emotions of fear and anger. He worked with Osment day in and day out, and in between takes, Night still looked like he was having fun.

"On set, Night was just very comfortable. I remember him sitting in a chair bouncing a basketball in between lighting transitions. He was a relaxed and comfortable guy to be around," said Osment in an interview with the *Hollywood Reporter* in 2019.

Mischa Barton, who played Kyra Collins in *The Sixth Sense*, also remembered Shyalaman as a studious, happy director who rarely showed negative emotions on set. He was easygoing and calculated all at once, making him a very brilliant director to work with.

> [Night] was always in a good mood. He's not the type of direc-tor who I remember seeing angry. He always likes to make it a good camaraderie on set. He likes to be involved in everything. He's quite studious, I remember that. I think he comes from a big family and they're all doctors or something, except for him. I remember one day they all came to set, his big Indian family, like nine of them or something, all different ages. [Night's] quite studious himself in the way he approaches his directing. He doesn't really get melancholic or angry or anything. He's usually in a good mood and really likes to play and use imagination.

In a profile released by *Men's Journal* in February 2019, James McAvoy talked about working with M. Night Shyamalan on *Glass* and *Split*, telling the interviewer, Ed Caesar, that Night was one of the most "prepared" directors he's ever worked with. In both films, McAvoy plays a man with Dissociative Identity Disorder, a mental health condition which causes a person to develop multiple per-sonalities in response to dealing with memories of trauma. He has superhuman strength and is a criminal, in *Split* kidnapping young girls. When filming, McAvoy said he was in good hands with Shya-malan's expertise and preparedness. He told *Men's Journal*:

> Night is kind of up there with some of the most prepared direc-tors that I've ever worked with. Him, Joe Wright, Eran Creevy, John Baird, they really know how to maximize what they've got and how to get what they need to get. Sometimes you get on set and nobody really knows what we're looking for. They sort of fart about for hours and hours and hours until we sort of get something that we think might be cool. And then you have 20 options of stuff that you think might be cool. And then they

edit it together in the editing suite and they go "Oh, yeah, that one, that's a cool one." and then, on to the next scene. But with [Night], it's way more deliberate and focused, which I love.

Night's *Old*, released in 2021, features Gael Garcia Bernal, who plays a father trapped on an island with his family that starts making the crew age rapidly. Bernal stars opposite Alex Wolff, known for his work in *Hereditary* by filmmaker Ari Aster, and Vicky Krieps, who recently starred in *Phantom Thread*, with Daniel Day Lewis, the megastar's final movie. In *Old*, Night shot the film in the Dominican Republic in a resort and on a beach, where the vacationers all start to age rapidly and violently turn against each other. Shyamalan typically sets his films in Philadelphia, where the weather is usually predictable and not intense. While shooting *Old*, however, he was challenged by wind and storms which would make it more difficult to get the right shot. Even with this challenge, he succeeded and remained calm the whole way through.

"The thing that I am really fascinated by how Night works. He's got a great capacity of being assertive which is something that is so useful and so necessary. He's always trying to dissect the specificity that's needed, in a way, because that specificity opens up for the ambiguity or for the complexity of the characters and of the story," said Bernal in a behind-the-scenes documentary by FilmIsNow on YouTube.

This kind of work ethic and precision can be seen in Shyamalan's direction of *The Sixth Sense* as well, especially with Toni Collette and Haley Joel Osment in the car scene. In this, Shyamalan worked with Collette as the actress reacted to Haley Joel's statements about seeing the dead at first with fear and disbelief, and then with sadness, relief, and emotional overwhelm as Cole starts speaking about Lynn Sear's dead mother saying she was "proud" of her daughter. The specificity that Shyamalan wanted out of Collette's emotions gave room for exactly what Bernal talks about in this interview: "the complexity of the characters and of the story."

As for Bruce Willis, who has worked with Night on *The Sixth Sense*, *Unbreakable*, and *Glass*, he and the filmmaker have developed a friendship and working relationship that has lasted for decades.

Willis said in Kiselyak's documentary:

> [Shyamalan]'s a rare individual in Hollywood because most films come from modern fiction, a lot of remakes of old films, remakes of TV shows from the '60s and Night just makes these stories up out of his head. He's a great storyteller. He thinks in big pictures. Although he does think about individual shots, he thinks about telling the story with the camera.

All of the positive accolades given by actors and fellow crew members show that Night is truly a gem of a screenwriter and director, some referring to him as an "icon" or a "household name" by the time the filmmaker turned thirty. This was all because of *The Sixth Sense*. The screenplay was something special to all who worked on it. And when it came to figuring out what the twist would be, Shyamalan told Apple TV+ in 2020 that the idea came to him one night while he was sitting on the couch near his wife's office space.

> My wife was writing something. We were upstairs, we had an apartment where there's a little upstairs room where she has a desk and I was sitting on the sofa and I was like, Why aren't [Dr. Crowe and his wife] speaking? Why is this couple not speaking? What's the marital problem? And, "wait a minute!" It was like that. It came from character, which is what writing is. If you feel really great about it, the plot comes out of the character.

This "a-ha!" moment would turn out to be potentially the greatest idea of Shyamalan's career, which started early as he was more interested in filmmaking than his parents' idea of wanting him to follow in their footsteps as doctors. Shyamalan's road to becoming a household name has had its series of ups and downs, but one thing is for certain to the cinema legend: after the success of *The Sixth Sense*, he knows that he is destined to be on this path, whether it be filled with blockbuster after blockbuster or flop after flop.

Born in India to a couple of successful doctors, Night stayed in the country for a few months before the whole family relocated to Philadelphia, where Night calls home.

"My dad, when he decided to come to America, it was literally the American dream. He was like 'I want to have the American dream and I want to go to Philadelphia where the Constitution, Independence, the Liberty Bell' . . . that was his thing. He wanted to go directly to the source of the dream," Shyamalan told Stephen Colbert while on his show in 2019 promoting his film *Glass* with McAvoy, Samuel L. Jackson, and Willis.

When the family was settled in America, Night started developing a passion for moviegoing. At the age of seven, Night went to the movies to see *Star Wars*, which first piqued his interest in filmmaking, but it was really seeing *Raiders of the Lost Ark* at age twelve which sealed the deal. Armed with a camera gifted to him when he was ten years old, he started making little movies with family and friends acting for him. Despite his parents wanting Shyamalan to follow in their footsteps as a doctor, he chose a different path, knowing that storytelling was his passion and calling.

"I was at the right age at the right time. *Star Wars*, *Raiders of the Lost Ark*, *E.T.*, all these seminal movies of incredible artistic and entertainment value came out when I was so impressionable. And so, the world lost a really mediocre doctor. That's kind of how it started," Shyamalan told Film4 for a YouTube documentary in January 2020.

In his early teens, Shyamalan was blown away by *The Exorcist*, which he was shocked that his parents even let him watch at that age. He spent the next month "traumatized," having nightmares and sleeping in his parents' room. This sparked a teenaged Shyamalan to become interested in making up his own scary stories to frighten his younger cousins who were still in their preteens. Shyamalan is surely a natural when it comes to frightening and shocking anyone who dares to listen to his spooky stories.

Shyamalan told *Variety*'s Jenelle Riley during an interview in 2021:

> Since I was a little kid I was always trying to scare my cousins, so I think this is a professional extension of that instinct. [My cousins] are all in therapy now, but it was fun while it lasted. I was merciless, on the verge of unkindness. My cousin comes from India and I convinced him I was possessed or we'd have two different remote controls for the TV and we'd do the Ouija board and the TV would keep turning on. He'd be crying. It was awful. And then I did a whole serial killer thing, there was a serial killer loose. It was fun. It would get right to the point where they would go "I'm gonna tell my mom" and then we'd be like, "No, no, no, I was just kidding, don't tell them." Then, the aunts and uncles would start yelling at me.

It took the Shyamalan family a few years to acclimate to American culture, waiting to get their Christmas trees and hoping that Night would follow in his family's footsteps by going to medical school. This, however, was not the destined trajectory for Night, who would spend his time in high school filming movies with friends and family. On one occasion, Night accompanied fourteen family members to the airport, and while he waited for them to board the plane, he saw a book about the making of *She's Gotta Have It* by Spike Lee. He begged his father to get it for him, and he did. Night said in an interview with John Dugan of the Aspen Institute that this book solidified Night's professional trajectory to become a revolutionary filmmaker rather than a doctor, which had at that point run in the family. When it came time for Night to apply to colleges, he went against what his parents and other family members did and applied to only one school: NYU Tisch School of the Arts. He was accepted and given two scholarships. When he went to his father to share the good news, the doctor didn't even look at him, uttering a small "Okay," which Night took to mean that his father thought his creative son was making the wrong decision.

"It would have been the equivalent if I said I wanted to start a goth rock band or something," Shyamalan told Colbert of his parents' reaction to his acceptance to Tisch. "All my aunts and uncles are doctors, my parents are doctors."

Shyamalan's film school experience lasted a little over three years and ended with the young student making his first film at the age of twenty-one. The movie was shot in Chennai, India, and lasted only a few weeks in two theaters before being pulled altogether. *Praying with Anger,* starring Shyamalan himself, follows a young Indian man named Dev (played by Shyamalan) who returns to the country for an exchange program after experiencing life in America. Night delves into the cultural differences and prejudice that Dev experiences with bullies and teachers at his school and displays how different the cultures are and how tough it is for an American-Indian to fit into India without being judged.

After his debut flopped, he got to work on his second film, *Wide Awake,* starring Denis Leary and Rosie O'Donnell. The comedy, about a young Catholic school boy looking to find God and the answers to the universe and death after the passing of his grandfather (played by Robert Loggia), was pulled from a handful of theaters in a couple of weeks and "despised by critics." The comedy still managed to be nominated for "Best Family Feature – Drama" and "Best Performance in a Feature Film – Leading Young Actor" at the 1999 Young Artist Awards.

And then came *The Sixth Sense*. Released in 1999, the film's twist ending stunned early viewers and the success pushed Shyamalan into the limelight. While speaking at Drexel University's commencement ceremony in 2018, Shyamalan said that no one thought *The Sixth Sense* would work, but after countless drafts and the casting of Bruce Willis alongside rising star Toni Collette, the film grossed massive numbers upon its release and subsequently shot the late twenty-year-old Shyamalan into stardom.

Scott Tobias of *The Guardian* reflected on the success of *The Sixth Sense* in a 2019 article about Shyamalan and the film, saying that *The Sixth Sense*, for a young Shyamalan, was abundantly important in order for the writer/director to successfully follow his peers in Hollywood.

> For Shyamalan, it was a last chance to define himself as Steven Spielberg's heir apparent after stalling out twice with *Praying for Anger*, his forgotten 1992 directorial debut, and *Wide Awake*, a Denis Leary/Dana Delany/Rosie O'Donnell dramedy that bombed in 1998 after three years of reshoots, edits and general psychological torment under the Miramax chief Harvey Weinstein. He even had Spielberg's producing partners, Frank Marshall and Kathleen Kennedy, along for the ride. He never lacked for confidence—in fact, it was his confidence that reportedly rankled Weinstein—but *The Sixth Sense* feels so much like the first M. Night Shyamalan film, in style and tone and twistiness, it's as if his previous work never happened at all. Like a true movie magician, he made his career struggles disappear.

Spielberg would even recognize Shyamalan's talent after the release of *The Sixth Sense*, going up to him and then-chairman of Disney Joe Roth to praise the young director for his work on the horror thriller.

Roth recalled:

> Every once in while there's a movie that turns out to be magic
> and you can't figure out what the movie's going to be. You can't
> know when it actually clicks in and you say, "Oh, my God, I
> can't take my eyes off the screen." I wish there was a formula that
> makes a movie this way, but this was one of those movies. I don't
> know if Night remembers this, and I don't remember where we
> were, but I was talking to him and Steven Spielberg walked up
> and said, "Congratulations." Then I said, "Thank you." He said,
> "You're the first person who's figured out how to make the audi-
> ence see the movie again."

While speaking to thousands of college graduates at Drexel,
Shyamalan said that there are two ways to look at his career: one,
an iconic filmmaker, two, a failure. He has grappled with the two
ways of looking at his career for decades now. From hateful critics and bloggers to an early screener standing up and saying, "This
film sucks," alongside *Newsweek* declaring one of his movies "the
worst film of the year," he has battled public perception on films
such as *The Village*, *The Last Airbender*, *The Happening*, and *After
Earth*. These films were commercial flops and panned by everyone
who viewed them. *The Village*, a film which excited filmgoers at first
with its mysterious trailers and strong publicity run, had a finale that
was confusing, underwhelming, and not nearly as jaw-dropping or
believable as the twist in *The Sixth Sense*. The movie had a strong
cast: Joaquin Phoenix, Adrien Brody, Bryce Dallas Howard, William
Hurt, Judy Greer, and Sigourney Weaver, but did not match up to
expectations and was seen as a failure for Shyamalan. Same with *The
Happening*, which starred Mark Wahlberg and Zooey Deschanel. It
was a failure and flop even in the eyes of Wahlberg, who trashed the
movie while speaking at a press conference for *The Fighter* in 2013.

He recalled meeting Amy Adams for lunch before they started working on *The Fighter*, and he told Adams about a "bad movie" that he did. Reluctant to share which movie it was, he folded and told the press that it was *The Happening*, a story about a post-apocalyptic world in which the world's plants make the humans kill themselves. It ended up being too on-the-nose in terms of the symbolism as a commentary on climate change. Put simply: the plants are angry at how poorly humans have treated nature, so the plants decide to seek their revenge.

"[Amy and I] had the luxury of having lunch before to talk about another movie and it was a bad movie that I did," Wahlberg said. "She dodged the bullet. And then I was still able to . . . I don't want to tell you what movie . . . alright, *The Happening*. Fuck it. It is what it is. Fucking trees, man. The plants. Fuck it. You can't blame me for not wanting to try to play a science teacher. At least I wasn't playing a cop or a crook."

Shyamalan told the auditorium at Drexel that many critics see him as a "cautionary tale," after major flops, and yet, he is still highly regarded, trusted, and respected for films such as *The Sixth Sense* and *Signs*.

One film in particular, *The Visit*, a found footage comedy-horror film starring Olivia DeJongue, was entirely paid for by Shyamalan himself. He took out a loan against his house and paid for the whole film without permission from a studio. He told Drexel graduates in 2018 that six weeks after finishing it, he was "nervous to show it." He traveled to Los Angeles to try to sell it and every studio passed. When he flew home, he was sure that he would lose millions of dollars and sell it to video on demand, with no viewers. When he arrived back in Philadelphia, he told Drexel graduates that he and his youngest daughter grabbed a puzzle that the young girl wanted to work on. Shyamalan said he was "in a daze," but excited to do the puzzle with his daughter. They dumped out 1,000 pieces on the table and started. Fifteen minutes went by and they found two pieces that fit together. Another ten minutes went by and they found another. When they got to eight to ten pieces, they were ecstatic. "Why did we keep looking?" Shyamalan asked the audience. "We knew there was a picture. It suddenly felt intensely simple. I don't need to know the picture of my life, I just have to trust that there is a picture. Just find the next puzzle piece and trust."

This revelation hit Shyamalan hard, and soon, he was applying this philosophy to editing *The Visit*, piece by piece. When he finished editing the film, he went back to a studio who had previously told him that they would look at it again when it was finished. That studio was Universal, and when Shyamalan showed them the completed film, they bought it. When it was released in 2015, it was one of the biggest independent films of that year, grossing $100 million off of a $5 million budget—a huge and unexpected success for Shyamalan.

After telling this story to graduates at Drexel in 2018, just three years after *The Visit* hit theaters, Shyamalan shared his thoughts on the universe and destiny to the students by citing Epictetus, a Greek philosopher responsible for "The Enchiridion" (The Handbook). Epictetus wrote about what we as humans have control over and what we do not have control over. Shyamalan said that all we can do is produce what we are called to produce and we are not responsible for the way our work is received. We are not responsible for how the universe presents victories or losses in our lives. All we are responsible for is our actions, the rest, is up to the universe.

"At any moment in our lives we have control over countless things, including our thoughts, and that is enough," Shyamalan said in his 2018 commencement speech to Drexel University graduates. "When we try to put energy into things the universe has control over, it will backhand you and teach you otherwise. It is in this dynamic that we get confused, where we start to feel falsely powerless. If you write a song, put all your energy and emotion into the craft of writing the song and spend no energy on how it will be received after that. That's the universe's job. They may want you to fail on your first few albums, but find the exact right writing partner that lets you dig deeper and find that point of view that will change the world. It is none of your concern how the universe helps you, you just have to believe the universe is moving on your behalf to let you grow and give you countless opportunities to do what you are doing."

Shyamalan has been chasing the same fame he received with *The Sixth Sense* for decades now, and although he's put his blood, sweat, and tears into his films, he hasn't caught quite the same high as the success of the nineties supernatural flick. After *The Visit* in 2015, Shyamalan went on to film *Split*, in 2016, which grossed $280 million on a $9 million budget after Shyamalan, again, mortgaged his house for the sake of the budget. The story follows an aggressive villain diagnosed with Dissociative Identity Disorder who takes young girls hostage and grapples with his twenty-four different personalities. James McAvoy stars as the villain and at the end of the film, we see Bruce Willis reprise his character from superhero film *Unbreakable* to help detain McAvoy's character and save the imprisoned girls. Although not marketed as such, *Split* is a sequel to *Unbreakable*, and soon, Shyamalan made a third film in the series called *Glass*, which grossed $111 million on a $20 million budget, another box office feat for Shyamalan.

In a recent interview with GQ, Shyamalan disclosed his love for Agatha Christie, an iconic mystery novelist, saying that he was introduced to her while visiting cousins, finding multiple books by the author on their bookshelves.

"[Shyamalan] admired [Christie's] drive to write without stopping for breath or worrying about the reception of her work," writes journalist Mallika Rao in her 2021 piece "The Mystery of M. Night Shyamalan." "He saw readers' expectations of the author as she rose to fame, then realizing that expectation would be part of his career too, so he stuck with thrillers because others recognized the genre as a 'offering to the world.'"

His dedication to mysterious storytelling is recognized by cinephiles and common film viewers alike as Shyamalan rises to meet icons such as Christie, Spielberg, and Hitchcock, the filmmaker even going so far as to collect vintage Hitchcock posters to don the walls of his Philadelphia home with his wife and three daughters. Hitchcock, who worked with low budgets and stuck to simple storytelling like we see in *The Birds* where a community is attacked by avian predators and *Rear Window* where a photographer watches a murder happen in the building across from him, treats films like short stories with plot lines that have little complications. This is the kind of filmmaking which Shyamalan has been drawn to. When he remains simplistic, as seen in his storytelling with *The Sixth Sense* and *Signs*, he is most successful.

It's not hard to imagine that Shyamalan is a pain to watch movies with, as many of his colleagues have labeled him a perfectionist, very precise and calculated with every directorial step he takes. When he watches films and television shows, Shyamalan told *Collider* in 2021 that he always has a notebook where he'll "scribble down" notes to help him later on in the writing process. On *The Tonight Show* with Jimmy Fallon, he told the host that he is sort of a nightmare to watch TV shows and movies with as he always views cinema and television with a hypercritical eye.

"It's tough to watch something with me, I'll be honest," Shyamalan told Fallon in 2019. "The family doesn't like to watch anything with me. If they're watching a TV show and I come in and even if I don't say anything, I'm just judging the camera angles and the performances. I try not to breathe differently, but I'm like, sighing and I'm like 'That's not the right lens.' I just get up and walk out disappointed and sometimes I'll walk by and they're in the den watching TV and I honestly will yell, 'You're making a choice [to watch bad TV.]'"

Shyamalan's learned that following Hitchcock by working with smaller budgets has been his "secret sauce," delivering "the most unique and provocative product." Every script, besides one called *Labor of Love* and another that he hasn't named yet, have been made into movies. When discussing *Labor of Love*, he said that it has emerged "so many times" in his career, a couple of times with Denzel Washington starring.

Shyamalan told Collider journalist Steve Weintraub:

> It's not a thriller, it's just a drama. It's something that I wrote. It's a romance, essentially. It was the first thing that I wrote that actually brought me into the industry in a real way. It was so long ago. So, it means a lot to me. It's very emotional. At this point, it's almost a period piece, because it was set in 1993, '94. It won't make any sense now with cellphones and everything that we have and so you would either literally have to do it as a period piece now, from that time period. It's very meaningful to me. It almost feels like a novel or something that I wrote. Trying to know when to do it and how to do it has always been on my mind. It's a very meaningful piece.

His latest work is the home invasion thriller *Knock at the Cabin*, with Rupert Grint, Dave Bautista, Nikki Amuka-Bird, Ben Aldridge, and Jonathan Groff.

The film, released on February 3, 2023, has grossed $54 million on a $20 million budget, with Rotten Tomatoes giving it a score of 67 percent. The film follows a gay couple (played by *Mindhunter* star Jonathan Groff and Bel Aldridge) as they are vacationing in a remote cabin in the woods with their adopted Asian daughter named Wen, played by Kristen Cui. In a review for *Variety*, film critic Peter DrBruge writes that Shyamalan's famous twist comes at the beginning of the film rather than the end. Within the first half an hour of the film, we are introduced to four intruders: an elementary school teacher played by Dave Bautista (known for his role as Drax The Destroyer in the *Guardians of the Galaxy* movies), a nurse played by Nikki Amuka-Bird, a small-time restaurateur played by Abby Quinn, and a lowlife played by Rupert Grint, most famous for his portrayal of Ronald Weasley in the Harry Potter franchise.

The twist is this: the intruders tell the gay couple that if they don't choose one of their own family members to die, the world will end. The couple, held hostage by the intruders, struggle to believe the group for the rest of the film. In order to convince the couple that they are serious, Debruge writes "the four strangers threaten to sacrifice themselves every time the family says 'no,' using their gnarly-looking homemade weapons to bludgeon and chop one of their cohorts to death." Shyamalan's screenplay is based off of a book by Paul Tremblay called "The Cabin at the End of the World," with Richard Brody of the *New Yorker* comparing the four intruders to the four horsemen of the Apocalypse while discussing the themes as they relate to American politics today, where there are the staunch leftist liberals (in this case the gay couple) and dangerous, religion-based conservatives (played by the four intruders). Broday writes, "[Shyamalan] puts the onus on the liberal and progressive element of American society to meet violent religious radicals more than halfway, lest they yield to even worse rages, lest they unleash an apocalypse."

Shyamalan has worked with Grint before for the television series *Servant*, about a family who loses their thirteen-week old son, Jericho, and copes with the loss by caring for a doll that the mother, Dorothy (played by Lauren Ambrose) thinks is her real son. Grint plays Julian Pearce, Dorothy's alcoholic brother, who starts to realize that the family's nanny, Leanne Grayson (played by Nell Tiger Free) has supernatural abilities.

"I'd met Rupert as a child when there were thoughts of me coming on board to direct one of the Harry Potters," Shyamalan recalls in an interview with NME in December 2019. "He claims that he remembers, but I think he's rewritten that. He probably just saw some Indian dude who came to the set."

Shyamalan told Drexel graduates that he's been offered nearly every movie franchise you could imagine, including Harry Potter, but he'd rather stick to a "simpler form of storytelling," like he did back in the day for *The Sixth Sense* and *Signs*. In fact, the only times he has ventured into big budget CGI was with *The Last Airbender* and *After Earth*, which were both "commercial flops." *The Last Airbender* was a sci-fi flick that came out in 2010, starring Nicola Peltz and Dev Patel. *After Earth* was another venture into science fiction, with Will Smith starring alongside his son, Jaden Smith. It would seem that this particular genre does not suit Shyamalan as well as the thriller/horror genre, as both of these pictures failed miserably at the box office and on demand. CGI and hefty budgets do not suit the filmmaker either. The filmmaker is very much aware of this, discussing his low-budget sweet spot with journalists and aspiring filmmakers alike throughout his career.

"I will compete with all of those things: with the big stars and the big CGI," Shyamalan told NME journalist Beth Webb. "I make sushi—clean things. They can use a million ingredients, but I'm doing it very cleanly, even if I'm making a gamble that the audience might not want. With *The Sixth Sense*, I didn't use the norms of the time—its ingredients were from an older generation—so it doesn't have that dated quality. I'm doing it the way Hitchcock did it, just moving the camera on a stage and using old-school storytelling. More doesn't excite me, less does."

In an article written by Scott Tobias of *The Guardian*, he labels Shyamalan as "The Twist Guy," who, indeed, can either wow an audience or make them groan in agony, like *The Last Airbender* or *The Happening*.

Tobias writes:

> The virtues and faults of *The Sixth Sense* would carry over to the
> rest of Shyamalan's career, suggesting that he had found his own

formula for success and he wasn't inclined to deviate from it. He has occasionally bowed to the trends of the moment—*The Last Airbender* was his disastrous run at a YA-style Chosen One fantasy, and *The Visit* jumped more successfully on the found-footage bandwagon—but he's remained a self-styled auteur who keeps drawing from the same well. He's the Twist Guy, forever chasing the same sleight-of-hand that dazzled audiences here, but has mostly made them groan since. But he's also a sophisticated formalist, with a talent for slowing the metabolism of traditional genre films and creeping into the darker corners of the human psyche. Even when he's bad, he's singular.

Shyamalan is also a philanthropist as his foundation, the M. Night Shyamalan Foundation, established in 2001, supports grassroots leaders around the world who are "like superheroes" in their communities, moving the needle of society and giving back to those in need. These leaders focus on developing better education, getting access to clean water, stopping sex and human trafficking, reforming criminal justice systems, and much more. Current leaders include Julie-Anne Savarit-Cosenza from Zambia, who focuses on community empowerment, health, and education; Katende Stephen from Uganda, specializing in community empowerment, economic development, and education; Mouaz Moustafa from Washington, D.C. and Syria, with a focus on community empowerment; Ngor Majak Anyieth of South Sudan, concentrated on community empowerment, education, and female empowerment; Paul Dean based in Philadelphia, focused on developing education; and Raymond John, a Philadelphian focused on community empowerment and economic development. Together, the leaders help change communities for the better, closing the achievement gap and focusing on enriching the lives of people of color and those less fortunate. They travel and work with community leaders who have been working diligently to change their communities, but need some financial and practical help in order to keep moving forward.

"We come in and make sure that it's accurate that they did move the needle and we ask them what they want," Shyamalan tells moderator John Dugan at an event for the Aspen Institute. "Whatever they want, we give them. If they need a well for drinking water or to build a school, we support them."

The Foundation helps communities "lift themselves out of poverty and combat social injustice" according to the organization's website.

Helping leaders in communities across the nation showed Shyamalan the effects of the "achievement gap," which Shyamalan tells Dugan means the gap in the United States between inner city communities and white suburban places. This notion intrigued Shyamalan enough to work for five years with the foundation, researching the causes and effects of the achievement gap and how the foundation might be able to work to close the gap.

The data that came from Shyalaman's researchers showed that the problem is not the schools' handling of the gap, but rather what communities are doing to influence the gap before the students even enter the building. Low-income inner city children are told in movies, television, and in the streets that they are "powerless." They are told "this country is not for you." They are "pummeled" by "subtle messaging" that they are "useless," according to Shyamalan's findings.

As Shyamalan told Drexel graduates at a commencement speech in 2018:

> The system tricks us into thinking we are powerless and the system will give us power when it deems fit. But here's the amazing thing, the system is made up. The caps, the gowns we're wearing. Chairs, everything's made up. Our art, the length of a record, seatbelts not being on buses, bands leaving the stage and

coming back for an encore, the dairy industry is good for you, we don't know how to make electric cars. The laws, the electoral system based on protecting those states with slaves, it's all made up. Why not you? Why did you buy into this garbage that you are not the creators of this world?

Shyamalan used his research to write the book *I Got Schooled: The Unlikely Story of How a Moonlighting Movie Maker Learned the Five Keys to Closing America's Education Gap*, which was well-received by educators and leaders alike.

"Schools on the same block with similar students can post radically different results. *I Got Schooled* is evocative and will encourage educators and non-educators to debate the keys to great schools. A must-read given educational excellence for all students is the key to unlocking our country's potential," wrote Cami Anderson, Superintendent, Newark, New Jersey Public Schools.

Shyamalan's legacy as a filmmaker, author, and philanthropist has seen its fair share of ups and downs, but overall, his success professionally holds him above countless other directors as a household name in cinema. There's no end in sight for Night, as he continues writing and filming intriguing and suspenseful storylines with some of the best actors in Hollywood. Will he ever hit gold again with a film like *The Sixth Sense*? That much remains to be seen. But it will be interesting to watch each of his puzzle pieces fall into place.

Acknowledgments

First of all, what an honor it's been to write about, frankly, one of the greatest films ever made. Whenever I've told friends, acquaintances, and family members that I'm writing a book on the film, everyone, young or old, knows *The Sixth Sense*. M. Night Shyamalan wrote and directed a cultural phenomenon that will go down in history as being one of the smartest, most engaging, heartfelt films with a cast and crew that was dedicated to making it perfect. It took a village to make it happen, to make it Oscar-worthy, but they did it.

There are many people I would like to thank for believing in my talents and passions, from colleagues to editors and family members. I am so lucky for my support system. I've built a community around myself that makes me feel empowered, and for that, I am most grateful. I want to first thank my grandfather, H. Brian Thompson, who got me connected with *Variety* magazine under the management of Penske Media Corporation, which also owns big magazines and websites like *Rolling Stone*, *Billboard*, *IndieWire*, *Deadline*, and the *Hollywood Reporter*, along with *Variety*. My grandfather helped set me up with interviews with *Variety*, *Rolling Stone*, *Robb Report*, and *Women's Wear Daily*, to work as a staff writer at one of these companies. When I met Ramin Setoodeh (now co-editor-in-chief of *Variety*) for an interview, we hit it off and I knew deep down that *Variety* was where I was meant to be. Ramin said that they weren't hiring at the moment, but he was willing to create a position for me because he believed in me that much—that I was destined for something great. I started working for the magazine under Ramin and a handful of other editors, writing daily news stories, going to red carpets multiple nights a week, and working on oral history pieces, my "sweet spot." Along with Ramin, I worked closely with now Executive Editor Brent Lang on oral history pieces for films like *The Sixth Sense, Gladiator, Scary Movie, Avatar, Jennifer's Body, The Little Mermaid, Coyote Ugly*, and countless more. I interviewed Hollywood hotshots such as James Cameron, Ridley Scott, Russell Crowe, Marlon Wayans, Anna Faris, Megan Fox, Karyn Kusama, Diablo Cody, Haley Joel Osment, M. Night Shyamalan, and so many more over the year and a half that I was with *Variety*. Without Brent and Ramin believing in me and pushing me to be the best journalist I could be, this book would not have been possible. I am so grateful for both of them. Working with them on edits was always a joy.

Next, I would like to thank my agent, Lee Sobel, for finding me, reading my oral histories, and reaching out to see if I'd be interested in writing books based off of those stories. I was making coffee one morning and Lee's message popped up on my LinkedIn and my email and I couldn't believe it. I'd never tried to get an agent before and here he was, falling out of the sky and into my lap. Lee believed in me from the get-go and was enthusiastic about working together to try to get my work published in book format. Before this, I hadn't even considered writing a book, but who could say no to that opportunity? I called Lee right after he sent the email and he answered immediately—he always does. Lee found Applause Books, an imprint of Rowman & Littlefield publishing, particularly publisher John Cerullo, who was interested in working together on this book about the making of *The Sixth Sense*. I prayed every night to find a publisher and it manifested into my reality. I started going on the manuscript immediately and eight months later, turned it in to John for editing. Both Lee and John are some of the kindest, realest, most supportive people I've ever worked with. Meetings with John have been both lighthearted and productive and Lee has stood by me every step of the way. Working with both of them has been a blessing.

Finally, I would like to thank my family: Mom, Dad, Baxter, Gummy, Grandy, and Grandfather. My mother and father have always taught their children to follow their passions. They don't force their children into a profession, but rather push them to follow their dreams, no matter how big. When I wanted to sing and play music in high school, they supported me. When I wanted to go to Northeastern University to study journalism and music industry, they stood by that decision. When I wanted to work part-time at a flower shop as a florist, they encouraged that passion. When I wanted to take poetry classes, they funded that. When I wanted to work for *Variety*, they were thrilled. When I wanted to write this book, they were supportive. I am so grateful to have grown up in a household where passions were cherished. For Baxter, my younger brother, his light is so strong. He has been through so much in his life and still has an optimistic view on the world. He has not made tribulations turn him cold. Everyone loves him and rightly so, he is just one of the sweetest most caring people I've ever known. I want to thank him for being who he is, for showing me that it's cool to just be yourself. For my younger sister, Gummy, she taught me how to not take life so seriously and to enjoy and have fun in the moment. She is the funniest, goofiest, smartest, most driven young woman. She has taught me so much about appreciating art as she has been studying art history since she was a little girl. Even though she is my little sister, I look up to her so much. For Grandy, thank you for instilling in me an appreciation for the beautiful things in life. Watching her tending to her beautiful gardens and making stunning flower arrangements inspired me to take up flower arranging and plant care and I have been working for florists since college. Grandy is the most elegant woman I've ever known. She is a homemaker extraordinaire and another person who I look up to. For Grandfather, he has also taught me to follow my dreams, no matter how big they are. "It's important to follow your pipe dreams," he said to me once. I will be doing that for the rest of my life. He is the hardest working person I know and he does it all for his family. He wants his children and grandchildren to live beautiful, safe, secure, happy lives and works tirelessly still to make this happen for us. As I said in the dedication, everything I do is to make him proud.

And for the subjects of this book, I want to thank everyone I interviewed. From Mischa Barton to Haley Joel Osment to M. Night Shyamalan to Joe Roth and Rosalyn Bruyere, thank you all for participating in the oral history for this book. I am so grateful for your time and hope you enjoy reading the book as much as I enjoyed writing it.

Index

Photo insert images are indicated by *p1, p2, p3,* etc.